MEMOIRS de NOCTURNE

An Anthology

Quotes, Poems, Song Lyrics & Novel Excerpts

Abe Sulfaro

Introduction & Section Narratives by Sally Sulfaro
Memories from Family & Friends

ıllı wordeee

MEMOIRS de NOCTURNE: Copyright © 2018 by Abram Michael Sulfaro

All rights reserved. Printed in the United States of America.

No part of this book may be used or reproduced in any manner whatsoever without the written permission of the author.
Artwork and photographs are proprietary and may not be reproduced without written permission of the artist(s) and photographer(s).

First Edition

ISBN-13: 978-1-946274-18-2
ISBN-10: 1-946274-18-6

Cataloging in Publication data available from Library of Congress

Published in the United States by Wordeee 2018
Website: www.wordeee.com
Twitter: wordeeeupdates Facebook: wordeee
E-Mail: contact@wordeee.com

Design and layout: Emil Lezama/Martin Rouillard
Cover Illustration: Ryan Sulfaro

MEMOIRS de NOCTURNE

An Anthology

Quotes, Poems, Song Lyrics & Novel Excerpts

Also by Abe Sulfaro
The Antiheroes - Treatise of a Lost Soul

MEMOIRS de NOCTURNE
is dedicated to the Abe's foremost love,
the city of Detroit and its people.

Acknowledgments

Miss Shela, Detroit Rock City Photographer
Ann Arbor, Michigan
Photo of Abe on stage at the Token Lounge with Slave to the Beautiful
Introduction

Pennie Spence—IKON Images
Grand Haven, Michigan
Profile photo for The Goth Years

Richelle Jo Sieland
Las Vegas, Nevada
Artwork for 'Cold Sleep,' 'Life Flows,' 'King for a Day,'
'Black Desert Sunshine'

Ryan Sulfaro
Brownstown, Michigan
Cover Artwork
Artwork of large man on top of Abe in *Memories* section
"Three Twenty-Two" section title artwork
Artwork for 'Swan Lake' and 'The Moment'
Artwork in "Excerpts" (Antiheroes) section depicting Fade and the Black Rabbit

Jess Allera
Photo of Zombieland building in Other Writings and Excerpts section

George Boukas
Permission to use photo of the Temple Bar in Other Writings and Excerpts section

Michael Spleet,
2SnapsUp Photography, Detroit, MI
Photo of Abe on stage with Slave to the Beautiful
The Goth Years Section

In Lieu of a Foreword

The Longfellow poem below was found among Abe's college notes where he wrote:

"The relationship between form and content is apparent in this sonnet. It's as if he's striving to get somewhere but never does. He obviously had many regrets about his past and portrays this well. He was hoping for better days."

An auspicious commentary by the young man who would later write The Antiheroes: Treatise of a Lost Soul and the contents of this book, MEMOIRS de NOCTURNE.

Mezzo Cammin

Half of my life is gone, and I have let
The years slip from me and have not fulfilled
The aspiration of my youth, to build
Some tower of song with lofty parapet.
Not indolence, nor pleasure, nor the fret
Of restless passions that would not be stilled,
But sorrow, and a care that almost killed,
Kept me from what I may accomplish yet;
Though, half-way up the hill, I see the Past
Lying beneath me with its sounds and sights,
A city in the twilight dim and vast,
With smoking roofs, soft bells, and gleaming lights,
And hear above me on the autumnal blast
The cataract of Death far thundering from the heights.

-Henry Wadsworth Longfellow, 1842

The poem below is an impromptu composition by family friend and rock'n'roll aficionado Dr. Ted Fazzari. It was written during a wake for Abe at the Diamondback Saloon near Ann Arbor, Michigan on November 30, 2014.

Song for Abe

Enjoy the sunshine on dusty dirt roads,
The shade of dusky tree tunnels,
Ever to the hole in the sky
Leaving us behind
With wailing guitars
And the long song of sorrow
We celebrate life, grieve death,
But god has his own way
Of raising voices to heaven.

IN LIEU OF A FORWORD

The untitled poem below was written by Abe on January 28, 2014, just days prior to being told he had a terminal condition. It was a text message to Greg McFarland (Spam in The Antiheroes).

What happened to the days of fun
and adventure
When we were beautiful rogues
Prowling
Detroit
like pirates out to take whatever
could be taken
The flags now fly at half-mast
Time is no longer our ally
Life is a precious but fleeting
reality
that sobers us all
and dilutes even the most potent of rums
The anchors grow
too heavy
to pull now
So we sit
The dead calm whispers
of days long gone
and sorrows
yet to be had.

Index

Introduction	1
Abe Quotes	4
The Berklee Years (1988-1992)	7
The Country Years (1993-1997)	21
Three Twenty-Two (2001-2012)	29
Champion Eternal & Slave to the Beautiful (1999-2008)	119
The Goth Years (1997-2011)	139
More Lyrics	150
Other Writings & Excerpts From The Antiheroes: Treatise of a Lost Soul	201
Of Dragons & Music (2010-2014)	233
Memories From Family & Friends	236
Artist Quotes	247

Introduction

MEMOIRS de NOCTURNE was published posthumously by the family of Abe Sulfaro (1970-2014), Detroit rock musician, author and poet who left us much too early as if he was shared with us for a limited time, "leaving us behind with wailing guitars and the long song of sorrow," as family friend Ted Fazzari wrote. Abe left enduring gifts in his music and his writing. Following his death, we discovered the poems, song lyrics and other compositions that are included in this book. They were all found in the small loft where he lived over the Nuclear Lounge, the bar he owned in downriver Detroit.

In addition to Abe's writing, we found a short film, *The Way*, Starving Artist Productions in association with the Motion Picture Institute of Michigan, in which he played a central character. His personal effects when placed together chronologically, weave a rich tapestry of his life and the many musicians and artists whose lives and talents intertwined with his. The history dates back to the bands Stormbringer in high school and BosCats during college breaks and continues with the groups Baby Face Finster and Bad Dog USA after the golden years of country and glam rock.

Constants in Abe's life were his love for music, animals, literature and fantasy, most notably the adventures he created for games of Dungeons and Dragons. During his last decade and a half, he developed a strong affinity with the city of Detroit, particularly its menacing streetscapes and the Gothic subculture that he embraced as kindred. His affection for both is intensely palpable in his novel, *The Antiheroes*.

Compiling Abe's writings for Memoirs has been bittersweet, sorting through handwritten verses in many notebooks, some poems and lyrics scribbled on scraps of paper between lists of things he needed to buy for the bar, bills that were due and notes from French lessons. Others, particularly song lyrics, had been neatly re-copied by hand (the originals were not so easily deciphered) with the number of bars in each verse, chord progressions, sound equipment that would be needed, technical sound mix details and performance set lists.

Each poem, each song, elicits memories of this man of many layers, the idealist and humanist who was painfully in touch with his own fallibilities and the stark realities of the world around him. Some writings have been intentionally excluded from Memoirs because they were too personal, others because it was evident from the "other" handwriting that Abe had co-written them with someone very close to him…too wounded and sensitive to name and left anonymous here. You know who you are. We love and respect you…always.

Of note is the contrast between the poet's youthful, hopeful tone during his college years (Berklee College of Music, Boston, MA, 1988 - 1992), with a couple of exceptions including 'Cold Sleep,' and his later, darker compositions echoing life's disappointments, resignation to fate, helplessness against systemic forces, anger and loss of innocence. The later writings reflect Abe's continued passion which had become brooding, however some compositions contain a crusty playfulness and whimsy ('1992,' 'Five Words,' 'Underwater Love,' 'Like So Much Nonsense,' 'Untitled 10'). Others exude peacefulness and contentment ('322' written in the old family home where Abe lived for a decade after parents retired and moved away) and even fantasy-like beauty ('Swan Lake'). There were several years (1993 - 1997) during which less writing was done because Abe and his brother Josh were rehearsing and doing live performances five to six nights per week. The contents of Memoirs are arranged in blocks of years that were evolutionary and yet overlapping in Abe's life.

Abe had originally considered what we've used as the title of this collection for his one and only novel which was undergoing final edits when he died. It has been published as The Antiheroes: Treatise of a Lost Soul. A section of Memoirs contains selected stream of consciousness excerpts in the voice of Fade, main character in The Antiheroes.

We hope you find relevance and some meaningful truths in Abe's writings. In many ways, he wrote his autobiography.

-Sally Sulfaro, Abe's mother,   on behalf of his family and friends

ABE SULFARO, 2012

With Slave to the Beautiful at the Token Lounge, circa 2007

Photo by Detroit Rock City Photographer Miss Shela

Left, Abe Sulfaro (Michael Simmons), Right, Josh Sulfaro (James Simmons) of the James Michael Simmons Band, 1993

Stormbringer, a rock group during the late 1980s. Left to right: Josh Sulfaro, Paul Sulfaro, Abe Sulfaro, Scott Sulfaro, Kelly Johnson.

On the roof of an old mausoleum in historic Woodland Cemetery, Monroe MI, a few blocks from the home referred to by Abe as "322."

Abe Quotes

The quotes in this section are from Abe's essays and prose, as well as stand-alone thoughts found among his other writings.

People can either create their own reality
or let reality create them.

———•———

Yourself brought to justice....
It's a taste that doesn't wash down easy.

———•———

Grounded by what made me fly

———•———

There were times when I couldn't have survived without you,
even when you weren't here.

———•———

I ran and ran until you were out of breath.

———•———

I continue to go back to you,
not necessarily out of love,
but a need to throw myself, again and again,
upon this sword
until I am numb to its pain.

———•———

It's hard to know what to do when something is happening that you don't understand.
It seems as if invisible forces are at work in fateful ways

that can overrule even your best intentions.
Instead of worrying about things you can't change,
just focus your imagination on the best possible outcome.
Reality may turn out closer to your dreams than you currently believe.

———•———

It won't be long before too long is gone.

———•———

One wrong move and I'll break through your ice.

———•———

I've got tunnel vision so I don't see you,
turned up the music so I don't hear you,
iced my hands so I don't feel you.

———•———

We're born on a beach and then washed away.

———•———

You don't get the concept of friends being lovers.
You keep them separated, sheets and covers.

———•———

You're so smooth, I'd think you'd tear.
But when I touch you, I feel sandpaper.

———•———

When your head falls from the clouds
will your feet keep you grounded?

———•———

The flag should be red
from all the blood that's been shed.

———•———

We are the real unacknowledged legislators.

———•———

A devil's laugh, a fairy's cry.
My emotions are mixed, and you wonder why.

Left to right: Josh, Frank Vitale, Abe, 1992

The Berklee Years (1988-1992)

The poems in this section were written during Abe's years at Berklee College of Music, Boston MA, 1988-1992. These were formative years, his writing reflecting wonder and youthful innocence, especially during his first year. He was joined by his brother Josh during the second year as well as musician and childhood friend Frank Vitale who moved to Boston to experience life in the city surrounded by music in the company of his longtime friends. It was at Berklee that they met Martin (Marty) Fitrzyk, originally from Detroit but living in Florida. Marty later returned to Detroit where he wrote music for Champion Eternal with the Sulfaro brothers and performed with Abe in Slave to the Beautiful at rock venues around greater Detroit 1999-2008. Marty and Frank remain close friends, really more like brothers, to each other and to Josh.

College Graduation, Boston, MA, 1992

Journey on Newbury Street

Look out
Eye level with the tree tops
A street winds away parallel with a blue sky
Both come abruptly to an end at a building
This is a point of power
Relish it and let it soak into the senses
There's meaning to be found here
I've really looked in
Looked out to look in

There's a lady, she's crying
She's in my way
Do I help her? No
Mind your own business
Nothing else concerns you
Keep walking

This street is funny; I wish I had money
Everything here is too expensive
I'll just observe

There's an old man with a cup
He's saying something
Do I help him? No
I'm broke
Keep walking; you're almost there

There's a beautiful girl
She doesn't have much on
Do I stop and talk to her? No
She won't even look at me
She's afraid I'll hurt her
If she only knew the kind of man I am
Keep walking; you're almost there

There's the door
Do I open it and go in? No
There's nothing for me in there
And I'm still broke
I just want to stand here for a while.

Broken Rules

I've fallen in love, it's no wonder
Look at you, there's no blunder
The perfect image of a girl
You've broken the rules
What mysteries do you conceal?
The stars have fallen
Only your eyes remain for me to follow
Will you lead me true?
Or is there still time to avoid regrets?
I think I know you
Look at your face, complete beauty
What would I do if the magical forest burns
And leaves me alone again?
The birds would be without a home
The bees would die
What's a man to do when a girl
Breaks the rules?

Thanks

The sun is the giver of life
Light and warmth bring beauty
If I was the earth
You surely would be the sun
Giving warmth and light to my soul
In return, I give you the spectrum
Of colors that cast their brilliance
Across the earth
These colors are the reflection
Of my love for you
Bursting from the prism of my heart
When your light strikes its crystal
The colors of my life are loosed
Upon the world to give thanks to you
For giving your love to me.

All the Things You Are

You are
The moonlight upon the ocean
A silver screen, stretching, dancing
Dazzling the horizon
Enchanting, enthralling onlookers
Below and above the waves

You are
The fragrance of a thousand flowers
Each one in bloom
Capturing, captivating all who have senses
With the perfume of love

You are
The winds of March
Moving, unsettling any who cross your path
Powerful and shifting
Weaving through life
With heights and depths unknown

You are
The mountain stream
Running gracefully
To destinations with hidden beauty
Waters so clear and unspoiled

You are
The placid pool, raindrops creating circles
Rounding, rounding, round
Rounding, rounding, round
Flowing slowly down

You are
The sweetest day in May
That month of months
Days like these cleanse the soul
And people celebrate life
On days like these

You are
All the love in the world
In one boy's heart
His angel on earth and beyond
Rounding rounding round
Floating slowly down

Eyes of Green

Beauty is your mark
This portrait I've seen
Your eyes…
The color of spring

The color of life
Alive in your eyes
Sitting next to you
What a surprise

One cannot think straight
Looking into eyes so great
Two flawless gems, thatched
Beauty unmatched

Emerald itself turns to stone
Next to eyes, green eyes, your own

The Apology Ballad
(February 26, 1991)

Hair of gold and eyes like emeralds in a deep sea
To touch you is euphoria to these hands without eyes
What did I know of love?
I watched too much TV, read too many books
Again and again I ponder these thoughts
Of how I stampeded and stumbled about
And expected your love like it was some fad
I was a fool and the one to blame
For love gone bad

I realize now that love takes time!
I will try again!

To lose you would be to smother
I will start anew and maybe one day
Pass through the gates to your heart

This may sound erratic
But these things I say passionately
For this poem is sent to the girl I love,
A girl named Natalie

A Heart for Every Season

I love you year round
Like the chameleon, my heart
Changes shade with the seasons
And like the peacock, I wait
For you to notice my colors

It's Autumn and my heart
Is as red as the leaves
They fall in a swirl of love and wonder
About your feet...please tread softly
For they love you and come to give you comfort

It's Winter and my heart
Is as white as the snow
Perfect flakes falling softly
Flakes that melt upon touching your flesh
These are my kisses to you
Lie down and make a snow angel
Impressed upon my heart
A snow blanket will keep us warm
When nights are cold
The snow loves you and comes to give you company

It's Spring and my heart
Is yellow like the flowers
Blooming in the meadows
Gather a bouquet and place
It in a vase of water
The flowers love you and have come to provide beauty

It's Summer and my heart
Is as green as the grassy hills
Tread its expanse and breathe its sweetness
Its trees, glade and shrubs
The forest pines and
All things verdant love you and come bringing my devotion

Cold Sleep

I'm cold. I'm lying in bed. My window is open but I'm too cold to get up and close it, so I'll just watch the snow fall until I go to sleep. I'm dreaming there's snow on my bed. It's getting deeper and deeper. I'm getting colder and colder and the covers won't keep me warm. I must be awake. I must have been dreaming that I was in bed. It must have been the trees that looked like bedposts or my frozen clothes that made me think there were covers over me. The snow is still falling. It's getting deeper and deeper, but I'm not feeling any colder now. Maybe because the sun is starting to shine in tiny rays through the treetops and warming me? I love the dawn. I always rejoice its coming, but I can't seem to move right now. Maybe I'll get up later. Papa always told me I'd never kill a deer because I'm too noisy and can't keep still. I bet he'd be proud of me now. There's a deer only a few feet away, watching me. I wish I could pet it. It has cute little horns and a pretty white tail. Yes, Papa would be proud. I wonder where Papa is right now. He's probably wondering where I am. I hope he's not mad at me. Won't he be surprised when he sees my little friend. I hope he gets here soon. The snow is still falling. I miss Mama and Papa and my brother and I want to go home but I can't feel my body and I can't see now. I wonder if the little deer left. I wish I could see because it's going to be a nice day today but I can't and I feel sleepy, so I'll take a nap until Papa finds me.........

I am awake now but not in my bed and not in the woods. I am looking at the place where I was in the woods and I see Papa there, but I don't see me, just my little cap and boots sticking out of the deep snow under the tree. The snow is still falling

Artwork by Richelle Jo Sieland

Left-Abe Sulfaro (Michael Simmons)
Right-Josh Sulfaro (James Simmons)

THE JAMES-MICHAEL SIMMONS BAND

Top, left to right-Billy Hamblin, Bob Olds, Dan Oestrike
Bottom, left to right Michael Simmons (Abe), James Simmons (Josh)

The Country Years (1993-1997)

The following narrative, written by Dan Oestrike, was read by him at a wake for Abe at the Diamondback Saloon, Belleville MI, on November 30, 2014. The Diamondback was the home venue of the James Michael Simmons (JMS) Band. Dan was the bass guitar player for JMS.

In the early 1990s, the Young Country Music movement was starting to explode on the radio and in the clubs. I was playing with a band in Pontiac and kept hearing about these two brothers who were tearing up the Detroit country circuit. I also heard they were looking for a bass player, so I went to hear them at a nightclub in East Detroit. It was there that I first met Abe.

What I saw and heard that night was a band with great picking, killer vocals and a stage performance with a ton of attitude. It was the best thing I'd seen around Detroit at that time. We talked that night, exchanged numbers and set up an audition. I was invited to be a member of the James Michael Simmons Band and that's when I started to get to know Abe.

If you asked me to list four or five traits that best describe Abe, I would say he had a great ear for music. He was honest and hardworking. He was a risk taker and a natural leader. It was evident when I first met him that he had a strong vision of what he wanted the James Michael Simmons Band to be.

During those years, we worked on many small and large stages. We played outdoor festivals. We were playing five to six nights a week. As busy as we were, Abe kept a strict rehearsal schedule, some weeks rehearsing every other day if things sounded rough. I was always impressed with Abe's ability to pick the right material for our sets. He was never afraid to pick from all genres of popular music to bring something new to the show. He got very good at satisfying the country dance crowds, playing all of the current hits and making you feel you were at a concert, not just watching a bar band. When Abe sang, he had the unique ability to shift from some Texas swing to straight up Hillbilly Deluxe, from a Robert Plant tune to some Pearl Jam or MC Hammer.

Many musicians start bands without realizing that it is also a business and quickly run into problems. The band that Abe led was run like a business. He kept a full calendar, played the best clubs, and he always paid the band on time. He also maintained the sound system and did all the mixing until we could afford the luxury of a sound man. A commercial van was leased to get all the equipment to our shows properly. Abe wanted JMS to be first class...he was always aiming higher.

Abe lived his passions, and he had a family that supported and lived those passions with him. It is probably safe to say we had at least a hundred rehearsals at the Sulfaro home where the atmosphere was always positive. Extra places were set at the dinner table on most rehearsal nights. This was extended family.

I have many strong memories of Abe from those years, but one stands out that I would like to share with you. We were finishing up a gig in Ohio. It was a typical January night with sub-zero temperatures and snow was falling. That night I had a fever, chills and misery of the flu during our five-hour gig. I was so sick I was getting delirious. To make matters worse, someone decided to break windows out of a number of cars in the club parking lot. Mine was one of them. Windows smashed out, zero degrees, the flu and a hour drive home ahead of me. I went back into the club to let everyone know what had happened so they could check their cars. Abe immediately offered to put me up at his house but I didn't want to get anyone else sick. Without saying a word, Abe raided the club kitchen, grabbed his toolbox, and headed out to the parking lot. He pulled out the broken glass and started cutting up some visqueen he had found. Within a few minutes, he had designed and constructed a temporary shelter in my car so that I could stay warm on my drive home. The swiftness of his response on that cold night and his compassion still resonates with me after all these years.

In the years after the James Michael Simmons Band, I called Abe occasionally to help cover gigs or fill in for a musician who didn't show up, and he always was quick to lend a hand. With Abe on stage, I didn't have to worry, you got the best.

I feel lucky and grateful to have met and worked with Abe and to have had his friendship for over twenty years. I'll miss him.

The years following college were spent recording country music and doing live performances in the greater Detroit area with reach into mid-Michigan and as far south as Cleveland, Ohio. Even though country music was familiar and familial while growing up, it was not the Sulfaro brothers' genre of preference. It was the music that consistently offered a paying venue and provided Abe and Josh Sulfaro with many stages and a loyal audience while they honed live performance skills.

Country music in the Detroit area was kind and receptive to Abe and Josh Sulfaro. They formed a group known as James Michael Simmons (JMS), using their middle names with the maternal family name. The group was widely known with a regional following during these years. Their success was attributable not only to the talents of the Sulfaro brothers (Abe as Michael Simmons and Josh as James Simmons) but also to the caliber of musicians who comprised JMS: Billy Hamblin, fiddle; Dan Oestrike, bass guitar; Bob Olds, drums; Gary Seeger, pedal steel and Danny Dunn, pedal steel. Abe and Josh covered vocals with Josh on lead guitar and Abe on rhythm guitar and keyboard.

Russ Connelly, owner of the Diamondback Saloon, was extremely supportive, providing a home venue for JMS as well as the financing for Nashville recording studio sessions where the brothers recorded a CD titled James Michael Simmons. Songs on the CD included numbers written by a few Nashville-based songwriters, by an uncle, Jim Doe, two songs written by Josh (James Simmons) and one co-written by Abe and Josh (James and Michael Simmons). That song is titled "Livin' on Bar Time" (lyrics below) and describes the life they lived during these years.

Other songs on that CD included "Don't Let the Sun Go Down" (J. Simmons), "Someone New" (J. Simmons), "What Went Wrong" (J. Doe / J. Simmons), "Heaven Burnt Like Hell" (J. Harris / R. Garrett), "Love Will Conquer All" (A. Barnett), "Love Could Find Its Way" (J. Harris / E. Moles), "Honky Tonk Amnesia" (W. Schaffer), "In Her Eyes" (J. Harris), and "Love at First Fight" (J. Doe). All vocals on the CD were done by Abe and Josh Sulfaro.

THE COUNTRY YEARS

Abe (Michael) with Diamondback owner Russ Connelly

On Stage at The Diamondback. Above left: Gary Seeger.
Below left to right: Abe (Michael), Josh (James), Billy Hamblin

Backstage at The Diamondback
Left to right-Dan Oestrike, Josh (James), Abe (Michael)

Livin' on Bar Time
(James and Michael Simmons)

It's nine o'clock and I'm late again
Twenty minutes fast is where I should have been
Race to the bar and unpack my load
Guitar, boots as I head toward the door
Not much of a life
But it's the only one that I know

Chorus:
Livin' on bar time, that's what I do
Playin' music all night
Waitin' for my day dreams to come true
Sometimes it feels like a crime
Twenty minutes ahead of the world
But still runnin' behind

It's ten o'clock and I'm stumblin' out of bed
Last call song still ringin' in my head
Head to the door and shoot for the moon
My appointment is due
Pull in to park
And I'm twenty minutes too soon

Repeat Chorus

Artwork by Ryan Sulfaro

Three Twenty-Two (2001-2012)

    This section is titled with the house number of the family home in the historic district on the east side of Monroe, Michigan south of Detroit. Abe purchased the house when his parents retired and relocated to northern Michigan. He often referred to the homestead as "322."

    His brother Josh stayed in Monroe for a few years and then moved to Los Angeles. Both brothers continued their music however in different directions with Abe also taking a job at the local Ford factory and buying a bar in Newport near the Enrico Fermi nuclear power plant.

    It was during these years that Abe became immersed in Detroit's Goth scene and pursued writing, recording and live performance within the Gothic industrial music genre (Champion Eternal and Slave to the Beautiful). Eventually, due to economic pressure, he rented out the family home and moved into the loft above his bar, The Nuclear Lounge, where he wrote The Antiheroes: Treatise of a Lost Soul, between 2010 and 2014.

    The "322" years are packed with Abe's prose compositions, the first one below reflecting his contentment while living alone in his childhood home in the old neighborhood. This period of time bridges the poet's earlier life with his re-entrance into the world of live music performance and eventually with his personal mezzo cammin...leading to his reluctant acceptance of the mundane and his embrace of chaos and dark musings and relentless search, not for an epiphany or revelation, but rather personal life interpretation.

322

Lazy Tuesday at home near a bedroom window
A September cool breeze
The tree branches sway smoothly
Happy birds sing heartfelt tunes
And a small dog barks intermittently
Far-off melody of church bells, so reminiscent
Yet undefinable, and the toll
Of the bell, melancholic
The noontime siren and the sounds
Of traffic on small urban thoroughfares
The lonesome whistle of another train
On the east side
Never was there written a symphony so beautiful
And I'm irresistibly content

Untitled 1

I was rebellious
And I coughed up blood
To paint your face
You were mood swingin'
And I was singin'
Live it up. Love it up.
Suck it up.

Zarathustra

He dreams of the apocalypse
And lives life in color 3-D
On the verge of a vision
Nigh time to start a new religion
An equal times =X, he's divided the plus /+
A faith in you, in god we trust
Night born sentries reside in his head
Smarter than you, can talk to the dead
Approaching fast, the last that he can
He dies so young, but he was Superman

God & Clones

We're all made, they say, in the image of god
And once in awhile we capture those moments
Of forever and shine through for all to see
But you can only really count on you.
There's no future in this world of clones
Most willing to conform
To own a piece, but a piece of what?

We're all eating off the same plate
Being shoved in our faces

Tried to love

Tried to love
But can't fuckin' get it together
Wanted love
But can't fuckin' get some
Stability versus
A mobile heart
And I keep for some reason
A roaming eye and
A weakness for temptation
Don't wanna need you now
Don't wanna leave you now
Guilt like a shadow
Can't forget all the things I've said
Can't forget all the things we've said
You were unsure of
Those words
My words
That fueled the fire
Of uncertainty
I thought I loved, but
I can't fuckin' get it together
Wanted love
But can't get some

My Statement

The beginning:
How it hurt for a year
But I stuck it out
To capture the love of my life.
I knew one day you
Would find my sincerity
And know my feelings
Were true.
I love you more
Than there are stars in the sky and
No mortal man will ever
Be able to match my
Love for you.
I don't care if you don't
Feel this way about me
But I feel this way for you
And I'll never be able to
Love another woman like I've
Loved you.
I want you to know
That you are all that
I'll ever need and
I hurt you.
I'm a failure.

Red Paint, Black Hearts

> Dead flowers on the window sill
> I cut myself today, but it didn't help
> I wanted to tell you how sorry I am
> Blood is not a substitute
> And love is unrequited
> RED PAINT, BLACK HEARTS
> So much pain without you

The Moment

The warrior waits…by the wayside…of life
Mother Earth I have sinned
Where is justice?
The river stretches…by the wayside…forever
I have drifted long enough
There is peace in my eyes
It is time to die

The killer waits…by the wayside…of life
Sister Moon I have sinned
Where is justice?
The highway stretches…by the wayside…forever
I have driven far enough
There is murder in my eyes
It is time to die

The child waits…by the wayside…of life
Father Sun I have sinned
Where is justice?
The cloud stretches…by the wayside…forever
I have floated high enough
There is love in my eyes
It is time to die

THREE TWENTY-TWO

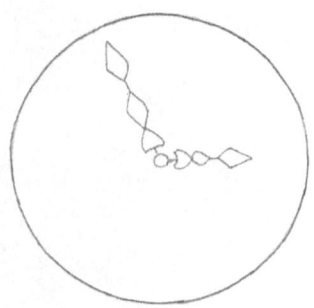

Artwork by Ryan Sulfaro

Rebirth

Rain drops
Streak down
My window
Like shooting stars

Not symbolic sorrow
But life-giving
Inspiration
Life-giving hope

Advent of the rebirth
Reborn with the rain
Reformed with the rain
Expiating pain

Flowers cannot bloom
Without the water, giving life
 Everything stops
When it's dried up inside

Not symbolic sorrow
But life-giving
Tears, tears, tears
Renewal has begun

Wishful Thinking

Wake me from reality
Set my alarm for eternal bliss
A bowl of unknown for breakfast
Death, the final frontier
And off to work we go

Confident Boy

I would never say never
So delicately clever
Or explicitly sincere
To mean every word

Daylight and the Moon

Seething in sunlight
Makes me feel a little better
I hang onto hope daily
Something to look forward to
How can one even live
Without dreams?

Glowering with the moon
Makes me feel a little special
Like I was chosen for this task
Believing I have something to offer
Be and you shall become
Do and it shall be done

Sparks will fly when I've found my magic
Never surrender 'til
I have made my peace
With Daylight and the Moon

The System

Born of love
You could die of hate
Let's wreck it for you to create
The system

Lookin' like this 'cause you're livin' like that
You can't change your life like you change your hat
You gotta do something with a brand new focus
Gonna pull out the tricks like a hocus pocus

Quit ridin' on the tray like a Ritz hors d'oeuvre
Gonna try a new way when I get the nerve
To change
The system

Painted People

Start this picture with the color white
We were born into this night
Now add a little red
More angry she said
Jump into your bag, pull out your brush
The color pink will make us blush
Wash it with blue so that we may cry
Dotting black so that we may die
Streaking the base brown, the color of earth
Growth of trees, the color green thirst
For life-giving waters, let's take a trip
Brush river azure, we bend to sip
Let's cross that line
One more time
Drawing a little faster
Past potential disaster
All we are, is the picture we've painted

Phoenix

Phoenix of fire
Sails through the ages
You know no enemy
On your stages

Bright as the stars
But you'll go higher
The Egyptians and Pharos
Called you Sire

Time is no concern
Nor restraint to your wings
Race through the galaxy
Eternity is but your slave

Messenger of destiny
The vision of worlds
You can never die
But you can never land

Time grows holes for you
Opening like desert quicksand
In a glass bottle

Like So Much Nonsense

I see this place
Where all around
We always look
But never found
Into this world
Underground
Upon the sea
The sea of mist, my love

In this darkness
We can abound
With life and death
All around
The seeds we plant
Into the ground
Will grow
Upon the sound, my love

Faces dance where shadows stall
In our cities, in our halls
Look unto our sacred walls
Watch the pictures as they fall
And run, my love

I see you in my garden
I see your face has hardened
Drown in my sea, and pardon
Keeper of the land, the warden

We've only just begun
In our world under the sun
See the eagle fly
See the eagle die
Like our freedom, soaring on high

Let us hide in the night
That shelters our pain
As it hides our sins
And sharpens our sight

Clouds of fire
Mountains of water
So much nonsense
Consider this if you bother

Fish in the sky
Deer in the sea
Living here with you
Is a fantasy, my love

Lizards crawl and blizzards fall
Serpents sneak and ships do sail
Fevers run high and temperatures soar
Feel the heat of my body
Pushing the oar

Off and running
No time to spare
This god means business
Come along if you dare, my love

Swan Lake

Her feathers are white with love
As they illuminate and play
Against the night of the sky

Her eyes shine like the stars
She dips and sways and plays
On the waves of Swan Lake

Not even time can touch
The beauty of her face
As long as she lives, eternity ripples
On the face of Swan Lake

Swan Lake is a place of magic
A place where stars always shine
A peaceful place for life gone tragic
The mystery that never lies

The black egret is filled with hate
And would steal the heart, steal the soul of Swan Lake
To bind her on the shores, in time
The lake would slowly dry

One lonely soul, one lonely boy
Sets sail tonight
The shores are so far away....
(In another place the reasons change)

One lonely soul, one lonely man
Steps on the shores tonight
Time has permitted growth within and without
And the black egret will pay

The heart of Swan Lake is free
One lonely man lies down to die once more

Artwork by Ryan Sulfaro

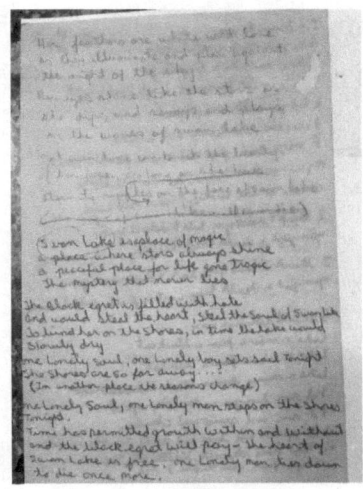

Abe's handwriting

1992

I left my love standing
Out in the snow
Nineteen hundred ninety-two years ago

Eyes turned red and then cried
Almost did I
As I turned 'round to say the last good-bye

What are you going in?
Said she right then
I'm taking a train to ride with the wind

And when will you call then?
Was her reply
I'll call on the morrow again and again

Untitled 2

You couldn't wait and give it some space
You never could figure out our place
On the road, a wild chase
I call and it's always a day late

What I see now is only what you allow me to know
What you do now seems only for show
It's not what you say now
But things I'll never know

Hold the phone

Untitled 3

There was never a time
When I would commit.
A train ride through murky plays
And hurtful ways
Like a slow death
And she finally says no.
The sun stops shining
And rain comes in torrents.
Now I know a weakness
That drains my soul,
A macabre dance.
I move without a purpose.
A sissy boy cries wolf
And she delivers the kill.

The Devil Made Love

It's got a heart that bleeds
But a mouth full of steel
Hip that breaks
And a hand on the wheel

You all know what I'm talking about
It makes a man do crazy shit
He'd never thought about

Cut it in
Cut it out
Take it in
Spit it out

The devil made love out of hurt and stone
He crossed the wires and cut to the bone
The devil made love out of thin cracked glass
For a heart that breaks but afraid to ask
The devil made love

Untitled 4

How does it feel
To crawl on your belly
Like a snake
Forked tongue lady
Cold-blooded baby
I need poison control

Oblivious Love

My spirit lies broken
But it's only a token
Of my fashioned passion

My heart lies broken
But it's only a token
Of my shameless love

I could care for you anyway
No one reads the signs
I would live for you night and day
No one reads the signs

I am shattered
I am shattered
I am going to be shattered
I am going to be shattered when
I want to be with you day and night

Enlightened through Murder

She runs through the hall
Her heart is pounding
And her blood races to her feet

He is right behind her
His eyes are death
And his sanity left long ago

Word fire is his name
Killer without consciousness
Or shame
Beast of the night
Taker of light

Run for your life
Escaping his knife
Bringer of pain

Has she lost his sight?
Her legs are aching
And tears blind her eyes

Here he comes again
You cannot hide from his fear
His silence, all that you hear

King of the Darkness
What possesses you?
Prince of the Night
What is ailing you?
Jack of Liars
Whose soul will you steal?

Ace of Fire
This world is higher
Than you will ever know

Winter's Reminiscence

His car was fast
But the season
Has past
Winter is here
With nothing to steer
The snow all around
Falls gently to the ground

Your stare was so blank
Death, brutally frank
Your tears, they freeze
Your face, the ice
Fills the empty space
In the heart and the soul
Of your winter wasteland

Falling!
This tombstone so cold
And the season is old
Winter will end with
Nothing to send you
The snow all around
Melts on the ground
Your stare was so blank

The Fan

> Round and round
> Spin, spinning
> Round and round
> Still turning
> Round and round
> Making that sound
> That hypnotic hum
> Round and round
> Still turning
> Spin, spinning
> And we sleep

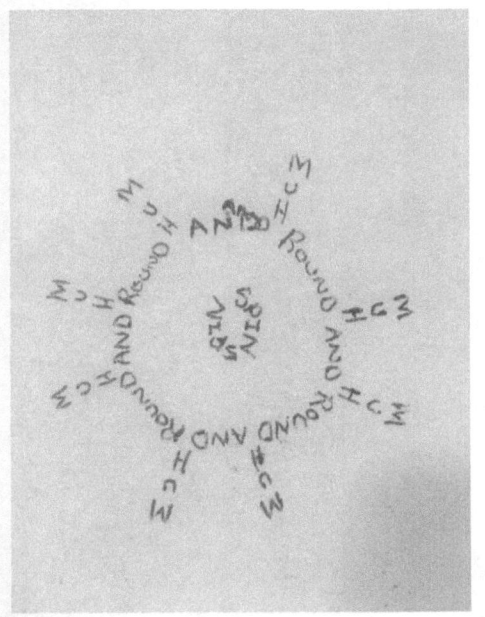

Sketch by Abe Sulfaro

The Dragon

Sail upon my sea
Walk upon my land
Soar upon my sky

Let loose my wisdom
Fondle my power
But wait…

For the hour
Rich or poor
The same is in store

Life and death
Are in his breath

When he wakes
He will judge all
Listen…

Unveiled

Your sweetest
Endeavor
Does proclaim
The rich and the reaping
All the same

Fortitude

Fortitude expresses
The deep desires
Of the heart that's twisting

Oblivion has
Become our escape
Faltered wandering
Into a land unknown

Terminal Tilt

Your eyes are the perceptual
And I am the cliff
Walk along my edge
Above the abyss

Careful… the line is crossed gradually
Once over it, no return
Mother Earth will be in tatters
Belatedly we scream our fears

Our hearts are the receptacle
Of precious things destroyed
When we die, our souls
Unable to protect and contain them

Who will save our brothers?
The givers of life?
Tall and ancient wisdom and strength
Have not prevented our time of doom

Waiting for Girls

Here I sit squalid
High up on my perch
Above a street solid

My brain is on fire
A lawn mower stings
Harshly in my ears...like a giant bug

The rhythm of my pulse
Pounding out my life
Like the gallop of a steed

Uncontrollable
Determination
And hope turns my head
Every few seconds
To stare like a corpse

Down the street I watch
All day looking thither
Still no girls come hither

Underwater Love

Last night
I looked into your eyes and drowned

Two emeralds, like swirling pools
I had no idea they were so deep

I waded...and then sank the fathoms
Into your heart

It told me the truth, and I drowned
Hearts can't lie for very long

Or hold their breath for very long either

Ready to Change

It's in the way you use it
So many ways to abuse it
It never hurt until now
The time is coming so soon
I've worked so hard and for so long
They tied my hands with my life
Who's the one that said I couldn't?
I could find out that maybe I shouldn't
But you're the one with with silver hair
I am young and ready for change

In the foyer at "322"

The Escape Artist

>Few and far and in between
>The ways I mean to tread
>I wish to be truly Free
>Every man's dream
>An impossibility?
>It seems the only door
>Is death...but even then
>Is one truly free?
>Even in death will I truly be free?
>Even in death will I truly be free?

Graduation Day

It is coming
The end of the beginning
Here is where I made or break
The life that I've been given
Phase four is on the floor
Time to live the big dream
Reality or fatality
Death lives in the ordinary
Insanity in the extraordinary
The politics of life
Bind and blind the unwary

Darkling

My only friends
The street lights
Have arrived to greet me

Night, my only true companion
Keeper of my deepest secrets
Has come once again

Tell no one my story
I could never face the day
Anyway

Dark intimacy will always
Trace paths to my fate
The life fatale

Abused, beaten and broke
How is life so unfair?
Look around

What has happened here?
I'm in control
In a world full of fear

Game Show

This is the new game
This is the new fame
Tune it in on your mind machines
It broadcasts our fate
So don't be late
The new order is about to begin

Watch the world spin
Guess where it stops
And you win…..nothing
NOTHING!

Nocturnal Talon

Cast upon high
Fly with all your might
Sail through the night
Finding life

Your wings so dark
The clouds will break
Upon your beak
Razor sharp

Your vision sure
You race the stars
Your talons clench
Upon fur

End did come fast
The fearless fowl
Flails into space
Death will pass

Station

I sit in the station
Look around
Even look down
To watch the time pass by

Where are you going, ask I
Somewhere important
Way, way down
To the City

Where are you going, ask they
Nowhere you'd know
Not a place
You'd want to go

But it's of utmost importance
To be in that place
It's nowhere
Down, down

Gadabout

The clock has stopped ticking
But his ways they are sticking
His hair like wire
His eyes on fire
His face the liar in all men

The wind keeps on blowing
But the truth isn't showing
Intentions are there
And the truth will but scare
Whoever he encounters tonight

You've trusted too soon
Placed your heart on the moon
Where he swore love lives

Gadabout, what do you pursue tonight?
Out to conquer the world?
Cheap thrills…
And your girl's broken heart

Summons

Listen to me
I want to scream
What happened?
I used to have it all figured out
Now I'm not so sure
I'm searching
The quest is never-ending
As years fly
Clarity dies
I'm so uncertain
Can't see through the curtain
This pale reason
In this late season
Is now like treason
Leading myself to the dream
So that I may be called King

Wicked and washed ashore
In this land of false thrones
Is there no escape?
The pain and torture
Of life is seamless
But is it schemeless?
Who holds the master plan?
It is buried in this land?
The wolves howl now
Their eyes are fierce

With hunger, piercing hunger
Only fire can stop them
They know everything
No lies in their lives
No notions or reasons
Only truth

The casualties
The realities
The fatalities

Their voices speak only truth
Listen to them call
Echoes down the hall
Your back against their wall
When they call you
You must go

Dream the Dream

Dream the dream
Until it seems
Until it leans
Until it clings to your life
Like skin

Expand this horizon
Infinite, the unknown
Hiding behind reason
It's the season
Lift the gate

The lake, the ancient lake
Its water waits
Points of power
Mark the hour
When the dream IS

Take us, shake us
But never, ever wake us
Dream the dream
The wonderful scheme
Dream the dream

f.u.P.B.

The stars are bright
Why do I feel this way?
Deep into the night
I'll drink the moon's rays
Hoping to find
Tomorrow
The better day

The days grow short
With nights that sway
Another party, but always
The same array
Live for the action
Fight to stay and play
What went wrong today?

Run River Run

The moon is out
The man is smiling
Down upon my face
Tonight is the night
Powerful and electric
Tonight it is cold
And tomorrow who cares?

The man will guide my hand
The river will run red
As red as dawn
Her color is welcome
Her light is sheen
Run river run
As red as dawn

Reincarnation

Climbing
Through time's seamless scaffold
Of towering space
Only to find the doors
Closed and sealed in place

Golden dreams?
We've been cast out
The next incarnation's social order
Is a dead end street
Of bricks and mortar

Lock your door and alarm your car

Moving Violation

I'd like to arrange my feelings
Oh so carefully inside you
And place this symbolic dream
In accordance with your love
A moving violation
Of my heart

Prisoner

I've cried the last drop
Death can bring
This well has gone dry
As I await spring

Let me replenish
The fuel of life
Let me vanquish
The giver of strife

I spun like a toy
In a torrent of tears
As my love was taken
In too few years

These words are severe
Parole me from pain
And let me live on
To love once again

King for a Day

Once I was a King
Crown and scepter on my knee
Flowers in bloom all year round
Spacious castles, courtyards in spring
But what are these things
Without my Queen?
Is this life or can it be
Something real or fantasy?
Is it chance or destiny?
Is this what I was meant to be?
Nothing now without my Queen

Artwork by Richelle Jo Sieland

Vulnerable Venerable

My face has cracked
My bones are frail
I must walk with this cane
At this age, no need to sail

I've seen it all
And once was tall
But no one can tell
As I gait through this mall

Now I'm alone
A new kind of fear
My wife went before me
Just last year

But I'll be ready
And it'll be welcome
I've laid out the mat
For death to wipe its feet on

My Crystal Glass

I've seen you so many times
But always through this glass
I've looked through you in my dreams
And burned a hole in your heart
Where I could place my love

Haven't you felt my passion?
It rages upon this glass
Maybe it just can't pass

Oh crystal, my crystal glass I need you
Oh crystal, my heart could be the fire that feeds you
Oh crystal, don't let this feeling fade
Oh, crystal, my crystal glass I need you

I've touched you so many times
But always through this glass
I've made love to you in my dreams
And reached the depths of your soul
Where I could make a bridge to steal your heart

Haven't you felt my passion?
It rages upon this glass
Maybe it just can't pass

Universal

Eyes of a depth I cannot discern
Though I submerge there repeatedly
If I die today, bury me there
In the only heaven I've known

Dreamed of the universe, its many guises
I've jumped and hopped and skipped
Across its seams so that I
Don't fall through the cracks in its sidewalk

The mulitverse explodes infinitely
In every direction at once
But it's only as wide as your eyes are deep
Two pupils, my heart and my soul

I am the traveler, the dreamer
The achiever, the lover
I belong to myself and to you
Perfectly locked, within one band

Our trust and friendship, relentless
Unchanging for no one except us
The pair, the two that are one
Our journey to nowhere will end when we get there

THREE TWENTY-TWO

The great force has crossed our paths more than once
We do not ask questions, just obey the call
Together we drown in a sea of love
Then reborn to love eternally

Our blessings, the stars, those billions are ours
The planets our wedding guests

Warning

Follow me under
The ocean
To find the notion
We've all been waiting for

Mother Earth has
Cried out
What's this about?
I'm scarred and burning out

A word to the wise
We haven't much time
The world turns fast
This could be our last

Listen to the Earth
She's crying
What have we done?
She's dying

Listen to the Earth
She's not hard to hear
Listen, you'll know fear
The end so near

Untitled 5

Hey, it's been a long time
I haven't seen you
I'm not there anymore
I loved you then
You were immaculate
And I was a god

You said you loved me
And cried
I believed you
I believed in you

I don't know if I can do this anymore
I'm immortal now, eternal, forever

It was never true
It was never ever true

Golden Heart

I walked through the door and sat by your side
I knew it was over by the look in your eyes
Your touch so cold and this sorrow of being apart
Even if it's over, will you wear my golden heart

I have no use for a golden heart
It looks so good on you
Like a shining star to match your eyes
Please do keep it, no ties

Funny how people change
Everyone seems to now and then
Even you and I, and we're apart
But I hope you'll wear my golden heart

Version of Yesterday

A version of yesterday just happened today
I stopped by your house along the way
Then came the hurt like a wild stallion
Stampede on my soul
Tomorrow is always a word of hope, so
I prayed it wouldn't happen again
Who can tell the future anyway?
Just a version of yesterday

To describe this pain:
Tear out my heart with your hand
I prayed it wouldn't happen again
Who can tell the future anyway?
A version of yesterday just happened today

Train Ride

Onward brother steel
Plow throughout the land
Your wheels make stops
The whole night through
I cannot sleep
When I'm with you
Passengers you take
Prisoners you keep
Clocks work slow against your feet

The Last Romantic

I've paid love's price
My heart frozen in ice
I've been trying to thaw ever since
Now I feel stuck
Like a bolted stool
The last romantic
Ever the fool

Untitled 6

Crawl Scale the 4 walls
Damn Get by as I can
Barred I'm losing ground
I Quit Get on with it

Break down the norm
Fuck that shit
Punch up the quo
Take the hit
Kick. Kick. Kick. Kick.
Clock runs tic, tic
Movin' so fast what? Stop

One for One

They say they do it for you
They do it for the community
They do it for the city
They just do it for themselves
And they should
Because no one gives a fuck
About you or your plans
Your life is all you have
No one cares but you
No one gets out, no one gets out
No one leaves
You can only rely on you
No one else, no one else
You can only count on yourself
Inside, Inside, Inside
I can't fuckin' reach it
Pull it out, Tear it out, Rip it out

Untitled 7

You never said a word
Just fucked me with a cold burn
You touch me with hate, I yearn
Your breath is all I heard
You love me with a cold burn

Untitled 8

Dissect my life
Can't catch my fall
Black light, cat's eyes
See it all

What's right, what's wrong
But it's my fault
Dead weight and chains
Burden is what it's called

Sharp knives like sharp lies
Cut the heart
Beat down shattered dreams
Thought you were smart

What's wrong, what's right
Still it's your fault
Black light, cat's eyes
See it all

Dissect my life
Please catch my fall
Black light, cat's eyes
See it all

You point, you blame
Cut to my name
I'm so dead

Better than Everyone

You act like the world
Owes you a prize
You got a gift from god
It shows in your eyes
And you deserve the best
So step on the rest
How dare you talk to me
You lowly pest

You're too good for me
Nothin' more to offer
Than the ass you swing
And when your life is empty
Don't come cryin' to me
You think you're better than everyone
Wait and see

Untitled 9

To the victors the oil
No blood on our soil
Your gods are worthless
Your culture passé
Conform or die
Even if you try
Because it's all for the show
To keep us in tow
It's all for the supreme
Elite American dream

Wicked Life

I've heard this before
This wicked life
What's it take to break it down
What's it gonna take to break me down

Sometimes, once in a great while,
I find a small space and cry
It never seems to help too much
Welcome to this wicked life

Show me a house that's never
Known sorrow or pain
And here's your pass to paradise
From this wicked life

We've heard it before, this wicked life
Life's a bitch and then you die
What's it take to break it down
What's it gonna take to break me down

Night Greenwich Roughling

I give all that I have
But it's never enough
Just your excuse to take advantage of
Mine's an unwary heart
Be careful lest you die here
Stuck in the mire of love

Think of all the times I said I care
How I always lay bare my soul
It is a fragile thing that you share
And handle so rough
Look dreamily at me with your gentle eyes
But destroy me with your heavy heart
Dreamer, Dream on, Dream Girl

Untitled 10

There was a this

And upon some time there came a that

Which we will also call a this

Two this and a that

Would they come along and converse

With a strange chat

And so they stood or sat

With two this and a that

Mumbling some strange chat

Only to be confronted by them

And some who flew in on a stem

So free to talk to we

Now two this and a that

Stood or sat

Conversing in strange chat

While they yelled at them

For coming late and inviting who

Whom nobody liked, especially we,

But nobody brought I

And I invited you

Which made who, come to think, faint

Now two this and a that

Conversed with they in strange chat

While them stood or sat with

You and I watched

Nobody trying to revive who
But we looked on and made a fuss
Then guess what came over
And wanted to discuss
And oh no!
Here comes he, she and us

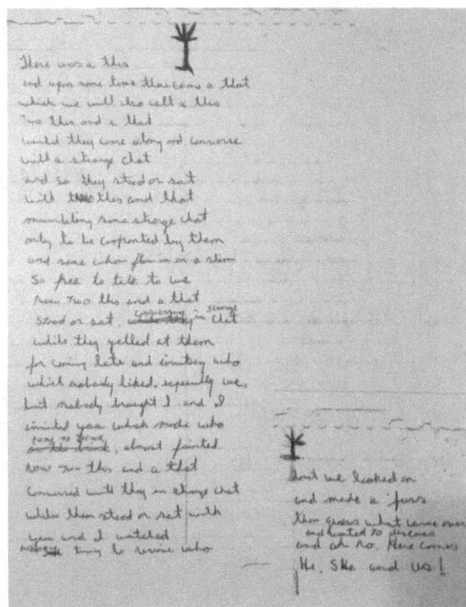

Abe's handwriting

Untitled 11

The river flooded
And the hurt came like a wave
Overflowing your life
You'd never be the same
What was the sense
Just a message and a lesson learned
And you're better for it
Strong like a mountain
Your heart beats fierce
No walls

Untitled 12

I was crying when I left
And the snow came
Falling from the sun
Like a tropical hail
I could never get through to you
Why won't you understand
I thought we loved
And gave a damn
I always loved to be with you
When you were sane

Nite Born

Bleeding eyes and a bloodshot mind
I couldn't find myself in the sun
Or the politics of ambition
Of the Day Born Gods

I need to run
I need to howl at the moon
And dance 'neath the stars
I need the creeping shadows
And the blanketed darks

I'm Nite Born and I shoot the world
I'm Nite Born and the world shoots me

Untitled 13

I can never get enough
You seem untouchable like the stars
The gleam in your eyes
Like the night sky, goes on forever
If I could capture your essence
And swallow you down like a pill
To hold inside me,
Inside my chest,
I would be sated
To have your love would be to know God
With this I would be immortal

Untitled 14

Live the future
Catch a star
Rise above who you are
Fall in love
With the dream
To let you know
What I mean

Untitled 15

Lookin' out my window tonight
Car alarms singin', cats in the cradle
The airport; 2nd flight
Thinkin' 'bout this time we said goodbye
All I wanna know, if it's okay if I
Cried this time

Untitled 16

Searchin' at the scene of the crime
Tryin' to put it all in order
The big spot light
Some things you'll never find
It's alright
Even when they're larger than life

Untitled 17

This is the new game
This is the new fame
Tune it in on your mind machines
It happens at eight
Please don't be late
The new order is about to begin

That Thing

Some call it spirit
Some call it soul
Don't care what you call it
As long as it takes hold

You can jib or you can jibe
You could be the best alive
But if you don't have that thing
No one will remember your name

Oow that thing, my emotional sting
Oow that thing, my emotional being
Oow that thing, do you have that thing?

Some want fame
Some want fortune
I just want to make
People feel emotion

Acquired or hereditary
Some people would say
What's it take to get that thing?

Lowly outcasts they were, they'd say
Before people saw their thing

Now they beg the secret of that fate
Now they rush to imitate

Who's got that thing?
Who's born with that thing?
Who's gonna find that thing?

It's few and far between
The ones who have that thing

Untitled 18

Little dark angel
Likes to sprinkle these thoughts in my brain
She never wants to leave
But likes to drive me insane

She likes the mayhem
And the chaotic jumbleland
She likes confusing thoughts
And walls of voodoo in my plans

Put the cross on and run me over
Put the cross on and four leaf clover
Put the cross on and roar like thunder
Put the cross on and pull me under

Cross my heart and hope to die
Stick a needle in my eye
Words of faith fell on deaf ears
Turn your lock and warn your peers

Little dark angel
Likes to spread these rumors with a flick of her wrist
She never talks straight
But likes to give my tongue a twist

Little dark angel
Likes to spread the violence with her evil smile
She never fights fair
She stabs me in the back and pulls my hair

Untitled 19

Am I just a selfish man
With an obsession for a plan
A plan to make my life uncommon
Listen to me, want to scream
What happened to our dream
Used to have it all figured out
Now we're not so sure

As the years did fly
Simplicity did lie
It makes just one thing certain
Can't see through this veil
Turns our reason pale
Turns about our only season
And then jailed for fucking treason

Untitled 20

Sittin' around slumped
Can't get over this bump
Don't know where to turn
Don't know where to learn
The answers I need

Can't decide on a plan
I'm a confused man
Actor, writer, model, musician
Man with no disposition

Suffer This

Good, clean, American mid-class boy
As stable an upbringing as could be had
You have a heart of gold, but nothing to say
Seems you were born for the masses
Without the magic of the outcast

You have your head in the clouds
Why can't you look around
You need to suffer this, suffer this
Be inspired by pain

Hopeless (On the Bottom Looking Up)

Longing for change
I can't seem to find
I know it resides here somewhere
Riding these undercurrents.
When will I stumble upon my life?

Apathy

Others must suffer
So we can sustain
We're just hunters
Who live on pain

Knowledge is power
But of little fact
We know so much is wrong
But refuse to act

Sit at your local pub
Sipping your suds
Talk about your little job
And who's next to blow your knob

It never goes away
'Cause we ignore it everyday

Machine

Gears grind, wheels forever spinning
Roll across the earth, unstoppable
Moving remorselessly and relentlessly onward
Devouring light, space, time, consciousness
A monster, void
Midnight gulf, Stygian darkness, the abyss
Nothing checks its progress
Until all is consumed
It moves unheeded by ourselves and the gods
Uncontrollable abomination
What have we done?
How many lives have been lost
So this edifice could stand?
This empire will fall
Civilization is not eternal
This machine must stop

Visionary

He looked into the room
With unbidden hate and rancor
Suddenly world equilibrium was shattered

They were not of the people
But an alien race
Their way, the way of death

The Great White Father in D.C.
Offers a peace treaty and land
Suddenly world equilibrium was shattered

You cannot give what was never yours
You can give land no more than
The air we breathe, the water we drink

The Earth is my Mother
The Sky is my Father

Smoke the pipe for blood
Smoke the pipe for love
Smoke the pipe for peace
Smoke the pipe for war

Today I have seen my death
Tomorrow I die, but I die free
Never would I surrender to the aliens

Killers

Stomp that spider
Crush that bug
People kill what doesn't look snug

Untitled 21

Blew by me like a motherfucker
SUPERCHARGE
I threw a rock, but didn't mean to make the dent
No more fucking accidents
I pulled the knife, but didn't mean to cut your throat
Bet you'd like to see me hangin' out on the rope
Who's gonna lay claim
Who wants the fame
Is there somebody to blame
I'm supercharged, baby
Lightning in the sky

Afire

Living to die
When I'm dying to live
Hangin' out in this world
But it just won't give

Birth of my death
Death of my birth
Livin' in this world
Cause a saint to curse

The world is on fire
I lit the match, hate me for it
The world is on fire
I add fuel, shame me for it
The world is on fire
With no water left, thank me for it

I could be your miracle
When the world is on fire
I push, if you don't pull
There's reason for the pyre

Birth of our death
Death of our birth
Wanna fight the world
Wanna end the curse

Untitled 22

The stars shone for a moment
Then the earth so drab, exploded
And sucked me down

You pushed me to the brink
And I went off the deep end
And I made a mistake

It was more, more, more
Than I could take
And now you're the innocent

The innocent, the innocent
And here walks the criminal
So subliminal

It's funny how, baby
You could turn it around
And watch me drown

You're the one who left
Gone, BAM
No explanation

I'm sittin' home
You're on vacation

Untitled 23

This business smells of death
You lyin' fucks
What's the point?
No one cares as long as
They dance, dance
Feel the trance

Take us away to another place
Our own private space
Where the moon roars and swoons
While you thrive in your shell
Your shallow hell
As long as we can dance, dance
Feel the trance

Dance in a trance among the ruins
So many words like melted butter
Meaning nothing

Untitled 24

The tears died, raining blood
Hearts spilled on hot pavement
No words were enough
To save us, only scattered letters
And fragments of love

Destroyed and crestfallen
Dreams died and flew on broken wings
Spirit ravaged, lost in a desolate summer
Life so sad, lonely is the night
How deeply can you hurt
And still believe in life

Bereft of hope
I'm pierced and encased in night's embrace

Untitled 25

Self-debased, denying the truth
Struggle with the weight that tightens the noose

Self-effaced, don't like what you see
Fade into the dark to set yourself free

Midwest Punk

Runnin' like the devil
Gettin' crazy down the highway
I'm a big hit, modern kid
I'm a bi-way
Lookin' for some action
Guns loaded, like I'm Kilroy
Never pullin' over, fuck the world
Let it destroy

You're the status quo
And I'm X Formula defects
Can't conform cause my blood
Doesn't run norm
Look at little Johnny
Playin' soldier, a GI toy
Here comes X with a spike
Let's kill the boy

Rollin' on a board
And some E, so pretty
Mohawk hair bright green
With a red flare
Combat boots hit the pave
Make a big dent
Comin' over to your house
Gonna stay and never pay rent

Comin' to a home near you
Tattooed blue with a big Fuck You

Late

Baby, it's late
I love this neon night
There's a mist, a rain
Comin' down like sparklin' lights

Hey, it's late
I can't stay another day
What a mistake to open up this door
It always rains on me

Last night, called you
Never home, stayed away
Looks like rain now
In my eyes and on my face
Dead inside, leavin' this place

Yeah I'm twisted up inside
Yeah you're leaving me unkind
You're twisting me and hurting me
The killing words keep time

Society Cynic

I am the cynic and don't give a damn
They've made me this way, the way that I am
Powerless to change, the vote is a scam
They are false shepherds and we are the lambs

Untitled 26

Life takes a twist
Life takes a turn
Thrown into limbo
Feels like I'm gonna burn
I pray I haven't gone too far
I'm killing you, you're killing me
Down so far I cannot see

Bleeding Rain

When it's bleeding rain
You forget your name
Unable to go on, so ashamed

When it's bleeding rain
You inhale its pain
A deep, unremovable stain

Untitled 27

You open up like a rose pedal
Welcoming the morning sun
Life-giving rain
Breathe, baby
Breathe with me

You open up like a rose pedal
Nectar on my tongue
Life-giving love
Breathe, baby
Breathe with me

Within You

Within you I feel my heart
Beating against myself
Smooth and steady
You are my anvil
As I pound out the rhythms
Of my life

Within you I find my heart
Safe and warm
Snug like a baby's crib
You are my temple
In here I erect my steeple
And worship you

Sweet Irony

It stumbles on you like love
Follows you like trouble
Stabs you on the double
Those who are supposed to, never are
Ones who don't look, catch a star
Sweet irony

You were ugly in school
The kids were cruel
In the rough, you were a jewel
Ten years later, you're a queen
Those who made fun, now obscene
Sweet irony

Don't look ahead
Don't look back
Fate's is a joker
And the deck is stacked
Sweet irony

Seeds of Deception

Thought I knew my direction
Til my mind was lost in your reflection
As you sowed your seeds of deception

Personal Jesus

I've got a personal Jesus
And 1,000 miles to go
I know I'll get there
But still trudging through the snow

Untitled 28

It's void, the truth
Yet I see so much
Look too deeply
Divine too steeply
Ride, Ride, Ride, Ride

Interstellar Devil

Walk the planes, ethereal ghosts
Solar angels, demon hosts
Galaxy deluxe, hyper-drive cruiser
Light speed ahead, no time for the loser
Warp and twist and enter the gate
Enter the rift, a soul to take

Champion Eternal & Slave to the Beautiful
(1999 - 2008)

Left to right, Abe, Josh, Marty Fitrzyk

Abe Sulfaro

Chaosium Studio.
Left to right, Marty Fitrzyk, Josh Sulfaro, Abe Sulfaro

Left to right:
John Avedesian, Jr.,
Abe, Marty Fitrzyk,
Randall Scandall

Champion Eternal & Slave to the Beautiful (1999 - 2008)

Champion Eternal was an all-original-composition hard rock group comprised of Abe and Josh Sulfaro and Marty Fitrzyk (Marty Seed), 1999 – 2000, producing one CD titled Chapter's End, recorded at The Chaosium, the basement recording studio at 322 East Fifth Street.

Some of the music and/or lyrics that were co-written by Abe with Marty and Josh are included in MEMOIRS de NOCTURNE: 'Black Desert (Sunshine Woman),' 'Angry 13,' 'To Be Immortal,' 'Child of Sin,' 'Killin' Me,' 'Chaotic,' 'Bombshell,' 'Deceiver,' 'Angel' and 'No Tomorrow.' Some Champion Eternal songs were later recorded and performed in rock venues around Detroit, circa 2007, by Slave to the Beautiful (Goth Industrial band: Abe Sulfaro, lead vocals; Marty Fitrzyk, lead guitar; John Avedisian Jr., bass guitar; Randall Scandall, drums).

At the time of this publication, You Tube videos of live performances by Slave at the Token Lounge, The Ritz and the Magic Bag are available online.

In Abe's words:

To me, Champion Eternal is more concept than entity, but to describe it in a practical manner, it is a person who is chosen by fate to bear the burdens of the world on his or her shoulders, someone who champions humanity against a catastrophic event. In doing so, this person becomes immortal, forever revered for the greatness achieved and the good that was done.

This is not an original concept. "Eternal Champion" was created by British sci-fi author Michael Moorcock who wrote about heroes. To me those heroes are symbolic of real-life role models--musicians, painters, poets and other artists who elevate and enlighten humanity--so I've used that ideal to inspire me to attain goals in my life. What one strives to do is different for everyone. Short of the lofty original concept, Champion Eternal status symbolizes striving to be the best at whatever one chooses to do. The rock band Champion Eternal pays homage to this ideal and to uplifting role models, those we believe to embody Champion Eternal qualities.

Champion Eternal greatness is always achieved through the medium of chaos. Truth comes at a price.

This section contains lyrics written and recorded at Chaosium (in the basement at 322) by Champion Eternal: Abe and Josh Sulfaro and Marty Fitrzyk

Killin' Me

You got it wrong
Down not out
Hear me when I say
Had my fill
Had to kill
Hate you still
God you're such a drag

Chorus
Killin' me
Killin' you...
Killin' me
I hate the things you do

Killin' me
With your poison lies
With your nervous eyes
With your sleazy sway
With all the pills you take
You're such a drag

Chorus
Killin' me
Killin' you
Killin' me
I hate the things you do

You cross the line
But this time
I'll put you in your place
Had my fill
Had to kill
Hate you still
God you're a fucking drag

Chorus

Chaotic

You call me evil, chaotic people
Would you believe I prayed in your steeple?
Open your eyes, candy suckin' flies
You see the world and it's crystalized

Pre-Chorus
Come on, come on let's go
It's gonna let you know
It's trippin', love the sound
And the world breaks down

Chorus: You are chaotic, we are chaotic

I can soothe you, yet I can bruise you
I'll never lose you
Let me show you how well I know you
It's in our hearts and souls to condone you

Bridge: You know my name. Am I to blame?
Chorus: You are chaotic we are chaotic

Now you can feel this, the world in half bliss
Except the righteous
Yeah, I'm gonna wake you up and make you know
That I am the King of Pain
And you can never hide

Pre-Chorus, Bridge, Chorus

(To Be) Immortal

You're so fucking chaotic
In retro exotic
What I want is erotic
And just a bit despotic

I've been awake 'cause I'm alive
I've been in love because I've cried
I'm never givin' up
I never wanna lose this life

Chorus:
    I've got it / Cryin' can't you hear me
    I've got it / Tryin' can't you see me
    Yeah, I've got it / Cryin' can't you hear me
    To be immortal, to be in love
    To be eternal, to be in love

Bridge , Solo
Chorus X 2:

Chorus:
    Our love feels despotic
    To live forever neurotic
    It would be easier to hate
    Unlove us, now too late

Chorus:

Deceiver

I can feel you, when you kneel, you
Make me want you, I gotta have you
And your feelings, I've looked right through you
Now you're captured by my voodoo

Stem aggression. Confide. Confession.
You are perfection

Your obsession, this will taunt you
And my possession, it will haunt you
I touch your mind, just like I want to
And your body, I feel what you do

You are perfection, demand attention
You are perfection

I'm your deceiver, and I will tell you
You're my believer, and this I'll sell you
I'd like to take you and then I'll make you
Take you under and this will break you

You are perfection, demand attention
You are perfection

This once was sacred, the union of the flesh
But now I've charmed you to make this little mess
You'll never know just how good you make me feel
You give me only what I can't already steal

Stem aggression. Confide. Confession.
Exile my tension

You'll never realize how I manipulate
Your emotions, and how I need to take
Your sensibilities, they are so fragile
I keep them all inside, destroy the world you make

You are perfection, demand attention
You are perfection

I'm your deceiver, and I will tell you
So many lies, you'll never know the real you
So many lies, you'll never know I wasn't true

Bombshell

You are my day, you treat me right
Yeah you are my friend yeah
You keep me high
So in love----love----love----love

You are my heart, with you I feel right
Yeah you are my soul yeah
You in the sky
So in love----love----love----love

Drop the bombshell X 4
With you I feel fine
Upside down or on the ground
Yeah you come to my emotional rescue
You keep me tight
So in love----love----love----love

Angry 13

I got a hole in my head when I OD
I got a demon inside, I'm gonna let it out
I like to paint a little face so I can be me
I wanna throw off the world so I can be free

Angry 13 Angry 13

I've got a feelin' inside and it hurts me
I got a demon inside, I'm gonna set it free
I like to paint a little face so I can be me
I got a 5th in the fridge, I think it's JD

Chorus:
    I got a knife inside that sets my blood free
    I got a world outside that wants to kill me
    I'm gonna put on this mask so I can be me
    'Cause I'm a bit insecure and I'm on E

Bridge: Red words on a white brick wall
We're kings of no faith but we're 10 feet tall
Black words on a red brick wall
Souls without faith, kings of nothing at all

Breakdown:
Angry at your life
Angry that you lost control
Angry at the world
You gotta let it go

Angry 13 Angry 13 Angry 13

Cut myself 'cause I'm numb to the pain
Dress in black 'cause we all bleed the same

Black Desert (Sunshine Woman)

Black sand on my city shoes
I gotta move, I gotta move
I see the stain on your bleedin' heart
Tough luck baby, bad luck maybe

You are the storm and I am the wind
Believe me I could stir your soul again
Take my hand, snake full of veins
Shake it baby, you'll make it rain

Chorus:
    Black desert sunshine woman
    Black desert, my woman
    Black desert sunshine woman
    Black desert sun...

Chorus option:
    I can't live without you baby
    I'm burnin' up in your desert heat
    Black desert sunshine honey
    Come on baby, make it rain
    Dance for me, honey, make it rain

Into the night you'll fly with me
Black desert society
Stained glass windows, adobe skin
Teeth through the vein
Leave the venom in

Cynics move out of my face
As I take control of your human race
I've seen you come but I won't let you go
I hold you tight, wait for the sun to show

Bridge:
Take me, take me down baby
Make it rain yeah
Sand storm on my bleeding heart
You put a spell on me

Artwork by Richelle Jo Sieland

Child of Sin

Drift apart from all that's there, from all that's there
You're actin' like you didn't care, oh yeah
You take it out on me baby
You take it out on me baby
You take it out...on me yeah
Uh huh X 3
30 years of empty stares
You sit alone but we don't care
It's weighin' down on me baby
It's weighin' down on me baby
It's weighin' down...on me yeah
Uh huh X 3

Chorus 1:
    I'm free like the wind
    I'm free like the stars outside
    I feel it within / You're shinin' within
    A child of sin
    There burnin' up the night / Just leave it all behind
    I live for one more time

Chorus 2:
    I'm free like the wind
    I shine like the stars outside
    I'm high like the stars outside
    A child of sin
    I live for one more time

Angel

You're such a dirty lover
You make me feel all special inside
Touching you is to touch heaven
Loving you is living hell

I can feel the fear in your eyes
I get lost in the maze in your hair
Maybe I should wear a disguise
So you can't see the heart that I wear

Above, below, she's my angel

Burning up, I'm doomed if I love you
Burning down, I'm doomed if I care
Maybe I should try to deceive you
Knowing you, I would not dare

Above, below, she's my angel X 2
She's my sweet angel

I can't ignore the feelings, I adore you
With my vision I adorn you like an angel
I can't resist the temptation, fall into damnation
Like a beast not the least oppressed, I'm obsessed
You're my angel

I would kill someone just to have you
I would jump the moment you dare
No one will stand in my way now
I'll trade my soul, the devil's heir

 Burning up, I'm doomed if I love you
Burning down, I'm doomed if I care
Maybe I should try to contain you
Knowing you, I would not dare

Above, below, she's my angel X 2
She's my sweet angel

What You've Done to Me

Look what you've done to me
I've been ripped inside out
I'm such a shell, a living hell
Wish I'd have died before I fell

Bridge:
Well on your way, it's so you
A street named Desire
And a face no one knew
With lingering cries

Look what you've done to me
You think it's all for you
I let you in, to breathe again
Now I'm on fire, I'll burn all we've been

Chorus:
One life is like there's no tomorrow
One life is like the last day on earth
Is the time still filled with pain and sorrow?
Then it leads me to my worst

You know I can deceive
You'll feel the words I say
It hurts to live in this light so dim
Never think this pain forgives

Bridge:
Well on your way, it's so you
With words I despise
Behind a face no one knew
With familiar eyes

Look what you've done to me
You know it's all for you
I'm such a shell, a living hell
Wish I'd have died before I fell

You can't, you, you, you can't get it back X 8

The Goth Years (1997-2011)

Left, Abe. Right, Greg McFarland (Spam)   Photo by Pennie Spence, IKON Images

Abe on stage at the Magic Bag. Ferndale, MI
with the Slave to the Beautiful 2007
Photo by Michael Spleet.

The Goth Years (1997-2011)

Abe's deep dive into the Gothic subculture in Detroit began near the end of his country music years. His brother hung on for a while after losing interest in the country genre, his decision to exit that scene compounded by performance fatigue (six or more night-long gigs and stage shows per week) and disillusionment on the part of both brothers with the recording industry. Josh expanded his music interests by studying flamenco in Spain and relocating to Los Angeles and later to Nashville. After Josh left the James Michael Simmons Band, Abe continued to perform at the Diamondback Saloon near Ann Arbor for a period of time until it was painful for those who knew him well to watch him going through the motions on stage. He finally walked away from it and dove headlong into the Gothic nightlife in the Motor City.

Abe told us that he first went to City Club on a whim but was quickly and seductively drawn into it, feeling a kinship with the outside-the-mainstream environment, attire and characters who frequented the almost hidden club behind an unmarked door off the Leland Hotel parking lot on Bagley Street. Abe's novel, The Antiheroes: Treatise of a Lost Soul, provides vivid descriptions not only of one of the largest Goth industrial clubs in the country, perhaps in the world, but also of the affinity felt by Fade, the main character and Abe's alter ego, toward the infamous City Club and the Goth subculture. That scene filled the void that was left in Abe's life after his years on stage, provided blank pages for the word artist, and dovetailed perfectly with the edgy music he preferred, giving life and voice, in collaboration with his brother and a few good friends and musicians, to Champion Eternal and Slave to the Beautiful. The compositions in this section appear to be poems, however some of them were written in a manner that makes it difficult to discern poetry from what may have been intended to be song lyrics. It was during these years that Abe developed a brotherhood with Greg (Spam) McFarland and Dayve (Disintegration) Watson who became characters in his novel. Both remain extended family. Fade, the main character in The Antiheroes, lives in these writings from the Goth years.

Untitled 29

The freaks come out at night
And I'm a ring leader
A loner with a painted face
Pale white, I come out at night
Androgynous, just for you
The city's straight from a sci-fi flick
A scar on the map of the states
Everyone here love to hate
But I love you
Gothic Detroit, Queen of Exploit
Everyone tears you down
I know the feeling
I'm your product, too
A freak in the Detroit Zoo
Who needs their love
When I've got you?
Detroit Gothic, baby
Detroit Gothic, now
Pale white, I come out at night

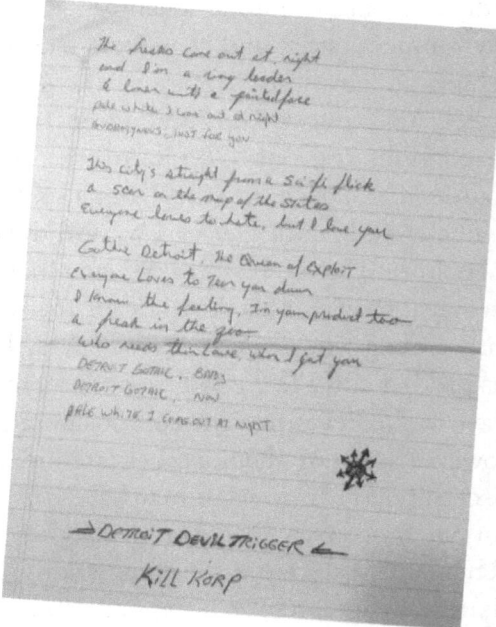

Abe's handwriting

City Club

Why do I sit in this dark, cold corner
Because I don't need you or anyone
To make me feel complete
My dark aura is power
It emanates here like a beacon
Hard like marble, this heart denies
So run amongst your social circle
Acceptance for the weak
This is not a sulk, but immersion
Metamorph, basking gloat

Go fuck thyself, I'm dead again
And so high, it feels so good
Admire me
I'm the one you should love

Here I'm the king of my dark world
This night is all for me, mine alone
Seldom will I bring another soul
So I can focus on my own and ours
I've become powerful here
In this magnifying room
You have to face all your demons here,
All your fears
Some grow weak
I grew strong

Detroit Super Rock

I am your nation
Your last salvation
I'm black contagious
I am outrageous
You can run here
But are you safe, dear?
The city's dark now
Shoot the lights out

Chorus:
> I am a loner
> And I don't give a damn
> The steam is rising
> And I see just fine

I am the best in a world without
I am the best in a world within
I am the king here
I am the Rock, dear

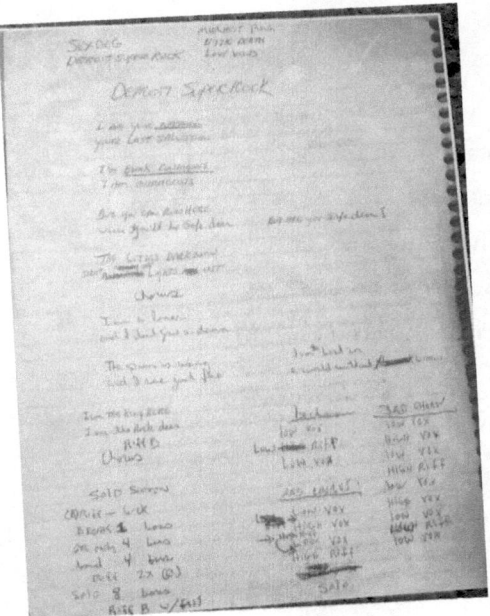

Abe's handwriting

Untitled 30

> Coke on Monday
> I'm on a rock trip
> Flyin' since Sunday
> Don't wanna stop this
>
> Coke on Monday
> I'm on a rock trip
> Need another payday
> Thru to Saturday

Vampire Hookers

Standin' in the burbs
It's a quarter to three
Shouldn't walk at night
But what do I see
Three hot Goths, waving at me

Feelin' like a hooker
Yeah I'm down on my knees
Vampire hookers
Gonna make me bleed

I wanna go somewhere
And talk about the weather
At the blood bank, baby
Get a little
Let a little
Give a lot!

Gothic Eye

I'm immersed in my own
Little dark world
I'm on the razor's edge
I need to forget
And escape from fear
The fear of failure
I cannot fail

They say I love the dark
Born under a bad sign
By nature, a malicious streak
I take pleasure in rebellion
Non-conformity, the left
Mysterious, anal, neurotic
Cool facade, my heart is still
In the right place always

Untitled 31

I am kin to OURS, the Gothic addicted to the scene and its dark serenity. The world stops when I am there. Live in the moment. For just a short while, nullify it all and be anything you want. Dream among the dreamers and OURS. OURS and the real world never mix. It's a stressful balance. I'm forced to split my face and the real me hides in the light of day during the week-long play.

Untitled 32

Put on my straps
And my polyester pants
And my platform boots
That lace up the sides
Grab my drugs
And do my dance
Welcome to my world
The living sci-fi
I'm a devil trigger on a mission
With private ambition
And I don't need your voice
On the other end of the line
You need secure, I need demure
I live in my head, live in my head
You think I'm dead

Untitled 33

She wears black and an evil smile
I don't give a fuck if you call her wild
Knee-high boots, little red horns
To know her is to be reborn

More Lyrics

As implied by the title of this section, it contains an eclectic mixture of song lyrics written during an unknown period of time. The ones that were co-written with Josh before he left for Los Angeles are from the early "322" years. Many of the lyrics in this section, judging from the notebooks and papers where they were found, appear to have been written during the late "322" years.

Devil Star 1

She got a strong right hook
She got a medicated mind
She got a pit bull smile
She got some dilated eyes
She got the one, two punch
That's frightening me
But she's all mine
Here she comes again

Bridge:
Hell of a time
But I put up a fight
Road block, nervous shock
Blurring my sight

She got a smooth forked tongue
She got a viper kiss
She got some jet black nails
And a wrought iron kick

She got some razor teeth
That's killin' me
But I won't be scared
Here she comes again

Yeah you're my Devil Star
Yeah you're my Devil Star
Devil Star, near to my heart
Devil Star, but always too far
Devil Star, shine on me, wherever you are
Lost in your spell, Devil Star

Devil Star 2

I see you in the crowd
Your smell is in the air
I taste you on my tongue
My hand is in your hair

I got you in my mind
I hear you in my head
Your voice calls to me
I won't be scared

Bridge: Here she comes again

You're all I see
I can't believe
How you possess me
How I can't leave

Bridge: Here she comes again

Chorus:
    Yeah you're my Devil Star X 2
    Lost in your spell Devil Star

I see you in the sky
Shinin' down on me
The light on my life
It's blinding me

Untitled 34

Come around the scene
Hard up, hungry and mean
Come around my door
Sleek and stealin', wantin' more

Bitch about my habits
Look, I gotta have it
Where do you think I learned it?
I know it's obscene

Chorus:
You're the drug I need
You're the drug
Want the drug
You're the drug
Love the drug

Tense down my spine
Need to rise and side wind
Would you rather have too much
Than not enough?

It's not bound by logic
More or less it's tragic
Played out, used up
God damn, you know it's tough

Battle Against the Gods

Why so jealous
Can you not blame us
For creating the conscience
Did we step on your toe
Disrupt the status quo
Drive us from your garden with your flaming sword

Satisfaction is a lonely thing
Live for your day
But breathe every moment
Sit up high in your cage and sing loud
Who would dare to strive for more than they have given

Chorus:
    I want a battle
    I want to fight a god
    Give me a battle
    I want to be a god

Who would dare to face their wrath
Unbidden I would
I see you, mortal
You're so blatantly clear
Go about your mundane
And we'll let you die someday

Fight, fight, fight them with all you've got
Fight, fight, fight them with all you're not
Fight, fight, fight them until you make
Fight, fight, fight them until they take

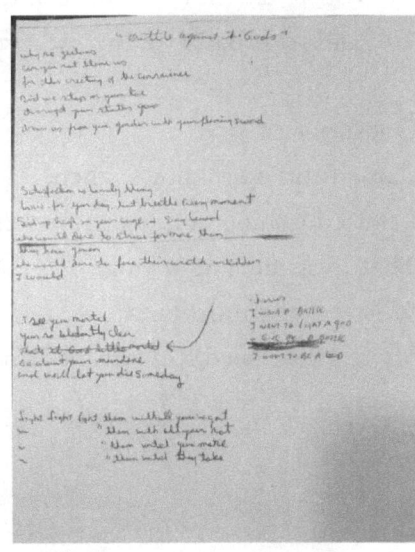

Abe's handwriting

Untitled 35

When I was young
Everything seemed so new
I never questioned the reasons
For what we do
It was simple to see between
What's wrong and right
It just seemed the day
Would follow the night

Chorus:
    Thank you, Mother, for nurturing me
    For life and breath
    And everything I've ever needed
    You've taught me that I can find if I seek
    And so I thank you for believing in me

Questions of why
Came from who knows where
I started lashing out, being unaware
That I was hurting the one
Who was the most kind
My fear and need had left me behind

Bridge:
Our relationship was the seed
To which you did tend
I'm glad you let me grow
Into a friend

Now I want to understand
Who you are
Your hopes and your dreams
You've kept in a jar
Can I ever give back what you've given me
A love of life and the chance to be free

The Truth in Your Eyes Will Outshine Your Lies
Co-writer: Josh Sulfaro

This place so out of control
A victim state now on a roll
Hate has been bred
War is just fine
Confuse and control
Don't get out of line

The future is black
They own the light
You've finally learned
Might will make right
Hate has been bred
War is just fine
Confuse and control
Don't get out of line

Land of Confusion
Co-writer: Josh Sulfaro

Staring at a blank page
Can't find the words to write
No fucking vision
No path to the light
In the land of confusion
Too many people, too many goals
Not enough time before you grow old

The burden of man
In a paradise
You're given the sun
You turn it to ice

The land of confusion
You run with the pack
The land of confusion
You give nothing back
The land of confusion
You're chained to the wheel
The land of confusion
There's nothing to feel

One of a Kind

She's got a strong right hook
She's got a medicated mind
She's got a pit bull smile
She's got some nightmare eyes

Chorus:
    Yeah she's mine, she's one of a kind X 4

She's got the one-two punch
She's got a wrought iron fist
She likes to bang it on top
She's gonna tie your knot

Summer Lights

The strip is hot like the coals of the sun
Steam shadows like a white ghost rising
Let's watch the rolling waves and seize the day
She said "The sun sets like a red world,
The peaceful hour when light meets night.
This is when we sail the shores of fate.

Chorus:
I see the summer lights shining through your eyes
Don't you see it
I see the summer lights shining through the night
Don't you feel it
I feel the warm breeze sifting through the sky
Take me

Let's walk along the beach by the moon
A walkway for the believers
We'll dance the desires of life on the ocean's stairs
Silhouettes like a masking of light
Come once again to set us free
Faster and faster we speed

Chorus, Solo, Chorus X 2
Take me

Raining Down on Me

Powers in the hills
So I touch the sky
Listen to my heart
Hear it cry

Hands to the earth
Feel her breathe
Drums in my head
Cacophony

Chorus:
    I can see it
    I can hear it
    I can feel it
    Raining down on me

Peaceful breeze
Turns to a storm
The sun goes black
The sky is torn

Lightning's hand
Grabs hold of mine
A flash of the vision
Holds my rhyme

Netherworlds
Of space I see
Spirits incarnate
Come to me

Here comes the rain
Here comes the thunder
Lightning bolts
Smote asunder

Sweet soul brothers
Please be kind
Give me vision
Peace of mind

Untitled 36

If you ever get lost
Where will I ever find you
I've been looking for love
But you don't think it's enough
You can't open your eyes
Even though it's all around you
Darlin' you'll never be alone

It's no real surprise
When the feelings won't remind you
You can't close your eyes
And make it go away
Don't blame your loneliness
On the people who surround you
Darlin' you'll never be alone

Chorus:
> You're alone but you never can tell
> That the season is right inside you
> Look into her eyes and take it away, yeah
> Do you see, did you find yourself
> Can you hear the voice guide you
> Girl you know, you'll never be alone

Can't you see the rain is fallin'
Will we know the time is right?

You're too lonesome to be by yourself
I can't make it with nobody else
No need to worry if you're sad today
There's no use cryin' on a rainy day

Saints & Artists

Spread the word
No, you're not dreaming
Let nothing hold you back
Courage is a rare commodity
All saints had courage

You see, the world
Does not reside
In another's point of view
Reality is a façade
All poets had vision

Chorus 1
    The dew line has been drawn
    A distant early warning
    Is now in progress
    Culture shock

Sing your song
No, louder than ever
Music can break all barriers
Passion is a sparse emotion
All musicians have passion

Show the truth
Splashed in vivid colors
Bear our souls for all to see
Truth resides in every frame
All artists have truth

Make believe
Yes, everything is alright
Faith and hope to a world gone awry
We need heart and we need soul
All actors have heart and soul

Chorus 2 X 2

We are the real
Unacknowledged legislators
The bringers of fire
Harbingers of the world

Divine Dissidents

All hail the coming of the new order
A new religion is being born
All hail the teachings of the rebel saint
A new messiah is in our wake

Chorus 1
    All hail the advance
    The final paradox X 2
    All hail the continuous emergence
    Of the God beyond God
    All hail the rebel saint X 2

It's time to mark the stones again
Ethics and religion fell fast asleep
The next victim to the lions we'll feed
Ostracized by society, so we can proceed

We always have a tendency
To repeat our mistakes
Who will be the next victim
For his vision burned at the stake

Bridge:
All hail the movement, all hail the advance
All hail the courageous, all hail the rebel saint
All hail the emergence
Of the God beyond God

Choke on the hard truth, sycophant
The status quo is never ultimately praised
It was always the insurgent
The blasphemous heathen
Saint and rebel have always been one

His name was Jesus, crucified for his faith
Joan of Arc, burned at the stake
Socrates, sentenced hemlock to take
Saint and rebel have always been one

Chorus 1:
New insights into the omnipotent divine
Their deaths raised us all to the new order

Chorus 2:
They rebelled against a counterfit god
In the name of God beyond God

Sinking Underground

I get up in the morning, look in the mirror
I'm forgetting who the fuck I am
Feels like I'm taking a piece of myself away
Every time I take it in

Chorus:
    God damn, you'll want to take it down
    Get on your knees
    Until you're underground
    Forever

Every time I feel you, I think that you love me
But you're just a shadow of my death
Feels like I'm taking a piece of my soul away
Every time I take you in

  Chorus

Bridge:

I know the devil, he visits me
Can't break me, can't shake me
He tries to take me, can't take me
At times I give in, can't give in, fuck him
Now I'm trying to fuck him

2nd Chorus:
God damn, I think I'm breakin' down
Bring me to my knees
I'm sinking underground
Forever

Resistance

An emotion like you've never felt
Feelings causing glacier melt
Inspiration like you've never seen
Heightening our vitality
Arming us against his breath
Giving hope in the face of death

Suffer this and suffer that
Forego dreams and forget plans
Futile lives with futile sway
You cannot stand in his way
He does not choose age, color or creed
He takes us all instinctively

Chorus
    Push back, push back against the night
    Push back against the fading light
    Push back against fate's injustice
    Resist its relentless might

We all remain slaves
Against the coming age
Persevere until it's done
Pointless now, what was won
Rage and struggle we spend
But destiny wins in the end

An emotion like your wildest dreams
Helps you live through the obscene
Inspiration like you've never known
Vital opposition honed
Arming us against our fate
Giving hope, tough it's too late

Chorus

Shape Shifter

This is your Savior speaking
I could be anything, anything I want
I could do anything, anything I want
This is your Shepherd speaking
I could be anything, anything you want
I could do anything, anything you want

I could be your miracle
I could be your miracle man
Just let me be your miracle
Let me be your miracle man

Chorus
    If you believe in me, then I'll believe in you
    I could be anything, anything you want me to
    I could be anything, anything you want me to
    Believe it rains or make it snow, let it thunder
    And then you'll know I'm your miracle

This is your Mentor speaking
I could make you anything,
Anything you want me to
I could do anything, anything I want

    I could be your Hate
    I could be your Love
    I could be your Life
    Coming from above
Chorus

A'Lectric Mod

She's A'Lectric Mod
In fashion's grand
My heart's a little scared
Looks like a demi-god
Not a semi-god
Loves her demi-man

She's A'Lectric Mod
In fashion's grand
My heart's a little scared
Feels like a semi-god
Not a demi-god
Love like sinking sand

Forever Sailing
Co-writer: Josh Sulfaro

I'm leaving here but I'm not leaving alone
Time takes its toll and I can't wait too long
Bow to your queen
Bow to your wasted world
You're everything, everything

You'll never find me 'cause I'm on my way
I am hurt but still I'll face today
Cannot break your chains
It never goes away
You're everything, everything

Chorus:
    Pale, tainted lover
    Love no longer
    In your life
    Left for another
    Light is fading from your eyes
    Save me again

It's never different but it's not the same
I'm on the sea of love
Bow to your king
Bow to my wasted world
You're everything, everything

I'm leaving here forever
It's been too long
I'm leaving here, forever waiting

I'm drowning here, I'm never
Going back that way again
I'm leaving here, forever sailing

Life Flows
Co-writer: Josh Sulfaro

I've gotta walk this road
I've gotta drop this load
I think I'll sell all my things
I don't need 'em anyway

Chorus 1:
    'Cause I been thinkin' 'bout this time
    That I've spent here
    If I could go back one more time
    Yeah time flows

Chorus 2:
    And I've been thinkin' 'bout the life
    That I've left here
    I would live my life this time
    Yeah time flows, time flows

I walked past a man
Spent his life on a plan
I said have you lived today
And then I heard him say

I never took the time
To watch my life flow
Now I'm blind
If I could see today
I'd live my life day by day

To see a child without cares
The old man stops and stares
So when your song is sung
Better hope you die young

Artwork by Richelle Jo Sieland

The Hunter
Co-writer: Josh Sulfaro

I am the blood that ran through your veins millennia ago
I am your peer, I am your protégé
I am the hunter risen from the best
Natural born killer, I am nothing less

Accept this sacrifice in the name of our blood, oh mighty father
It's you who has breathed life into my heart
And I am grateful and would do you honor
I am your blood, a millennium of power

You take me down through the blood line
To meet my father, blood of my kind
I am the hunter schooled from the best
Natural born killer, I am nothing less

Chorus:
    Your words are all in vain
    You can't escape the pain
    I'm coming on again
    I'll give this blood your name

Fade Away
Co-writer: Josh Sulfaro

Your reflective eyes show no sign of soul
Your mind is empty, emotions gone
Time did take its toll

Chorus:
Your eyes, burn out til they fade away X 3

Your lines are never right
Crack the whip, smash the dream
You wanna rule the night so you toil
Hands filled with pain

Your words are never straight, lost inside
Of your mind
Crack the whip, smash the dream
Don't get caught walkin' out of line

Spoonfed (Walking Dead)
Co-writer: Josh Sulfaro

I'm hangin' by a thread
When I'm hangin' with you
I'm on my last stand
With the things that you do,
The way I feel for you

It sounds so damn good
What they sell to you
Distorting all you view
It's what they do

Pre-chorus:
    Tear me down, tear you down

Chorus 1:
    You're feelin' drunk and stoned
    A king without a throne
    Their voice is in your head
    They love you spoonfed

Butterflies are flyin'
All around your head
The things you think you were
Are not what they said

Don't need to care for me
I'm on my own
Put your life in their hands
And they'll kill your soul
The way they treat you

Chorus 2:
You're feelin' drunk and stoned
Their rhythm's in your head
They beat you with your bones
You're looking like their clone
The wire's in your head
Now you're spoonfed
Now you're walking dead

What Is Freedom
Co-writer: Josh Sulfaro

Black hills, white crime
Peoples' hands held to the sky
Land deal, blood rains
Big business always gains

Chorus 1:
    There I was standing
    I wasn't dreamin'
    Left empty handed
    People were screamin'
    While they were runnin' away
    What is freedom

Our voice unheard
Decisions made without our word
Big town, rat race
People work without a face

Chorus.

Bridge:
    Now I sit and watch the clouds roll by
    Move across this big open sky
    What would it take to be as free as you
    How would it feel to be the way you do

Tax time, big crime
Takin' dollars and leavin' dimes
News flash, all trash
Tellin' lies, collectin' cash

Takin' land, makin' plans
To subdivide all they can
One earth, one chance
It's wake up time in wonderland

Chorus 2:
Now here we're standin'
No we're not dreamin'
Left empty handed
Tired of screamin'
But we're not runnin' away
What is freedom

Spirit Woman

Summer breeze on a desert highway
Searchin' for the man inside
Came out here to do it my way
Tired of lookin' for a place to hide
As I look in all four direccions

Wake from a dream in the middle of the night
I hear her call like a friend
Her writing's on the wall
Maybe it was just the wind
As I look in all four directions

Chorus:
    Spirit woman, I'm crying for you
    Spirit woman, pull me through
    Won't you help pull me through

Wander alone without direction
Following her footprints in the sand
Can see the smoke signals in the distance
Oh, she takes me by the hand
As we walk in all four direcctions

Wake from a dream in the middle of the night
I hear her call like a friend
Her writing's on the wall
Hungry for her soul affection
I turn around and see her face again

Fly away, someday she will return X 2
Gone away, I'm always hoping for her X 2

Til We Meet Again

Feeling strong, can't be wrong
Leavin' this town tonight
Pack my things, I'll spread my wings
It's my time to take flight

Bridge:
>You used to stand there and wait
>Unlike my dreams, hold open the gate

Chorus:
>So watch as I climb
>Where some crashed and burned
>Mountains so high
>Winds of fate often turn
>I know what I feel, but it is surreal
>Til we meet again

Seize the day, make your way
From the dark to the sun
Feel no fear, the path is clear
Our wants now have become one

Bridge:
>You used to stand there and wait
>Follow your dreams before it's too late

Chorus.

Til we meet again X2

Sailing Away

Standing here
With a picture in my mind
It's so clear
But it's you I cannot find

Set my sights
To fill empty space
To the sea
Feel the wind's cool embrace

Chorus:
Sailing away, sailing away
Sailing away til I find someone
Someone like you

Pure and clear
Deep blue sparkle in her eyes
Is she here?
Will she surface in disguise?

Shallow skin
The treasure of my pride
Diving in
Find the beauty deep inside

Crowd Creature

I thought I saw you for just a moment
When the eel slid down my spine
I bolted upright
And the crowd shifted tight

I looked around and I thought I saw you X 2

Chorus:
    It's so cold in the middle of July
    It's never been so cold, I might die
    I touched myself, like frost on a rock
    And bolted upright
    As the eel slide down my spine

I thought I saw you for just a glimpse
As the shiver made my teeth quake
I wanted to run
But the crowd tipped over

I looked around and I thought I saw you X 2

Chorus

My Hurting Friend

My hurting friend
I hurt you and I've ruined my life
Can't stand it, why I didn't think twice
All these things that happen now
All these things...I don't know how

Chorus:
Oh here it comes again
Oh here it comes again
Oh here it comes again
My hurting friend

Lost your love and I'm lonely now
Lost your heart when I shut mine down
Don't know if I'll see you again
Don't know why I lost my best friend

I hope that you'll come back now
I hope that you'll forgive me somehow
This feeling washes over me all the time
This feeling drowns me a bit again

Will I Ever Get Over You

Night time is the worst time
'Cause I'm lying here thinking of you
Sunshine hurts my eyes
From the tears I cried the whole night through

And all I can do is think of you
While somebody else is holding you

Chorus:
> Will I ever get over you
> Or will I keep on thinking
> I'll never know what to do without you
> Will I ever get over you
> Or will this last my whole life through

Sometimes it seems so hopeless
When I'm walkin' the streets of town
Need the strength to break the chains on my heart
So it won't be bound

And all I can do is think of you
While somebody else is holding you

Chorus

Bridge:
Sometimes I'll think of you
Feels like I'll never know what to do

Chorus X 2

Growing the Messiah

The babe is born so innocent and pure
Hide it away from all the imperfections
Including the taint of ourselves
Just give it food and water like the backyard dog
Nurture the messiah like you slop your hog

Chorus 1:
    Growing the messiah
    Come and fix this world
    It's come apart like a broken toy
    Growing the messiah
    Clap your hands, enjoy

Let him loose from his prison cell
To wander around this man-made hell
He's so perfect in every way
So naive, dumb, harmless, he can't talk anyway
Been free from the world all of his life
So only he can see how to undo this strife

Chorus 2:
    Growing the messiah
    Come and fix what we've done
    We're slowing dying like the burning son
    Growing the messiah, couldn't wait anymore
    Growing the messiah, apocalypse at our door

Untitled 37

Put a record on the stereo
Nothin' to do and no place to go
Leaving his old life behind

He said, "Lady, I've got to know
What it's like to be on your own.
Could you spare some time?"

She said, "Mister, it's enough to know
That sometimes life is a no-go show
And sometimes you'll find, she said…."

Pre-chorus:
It's just gonna take some time
It'll come soon enough you'll find

Chorus:
Then a light shown in her eyes X 2
It was a power she couldn't disguise

Fangs

Last night I awoke when you jabbed me
Sat right up, felt the pain when you stabbed me
Needed to save my life, but you weren't there

Sweat drenched down my pillow casing
Get my ass up, to start facing
Needed to save my life, but you weren't there

Bridge:
    Tugging my heart across the miles
    Pulling my soul, spilling your guile

Chorus:
    Needle sharp teeth, you drink your fill
    When you grow fangs, you sap my will
    When you grow fangs, you make your kill
    When you grow fangs, the blood will spill
    When you grow fangs, I love you still

Trying to stem this red tidal wave
Yet give you all that you might crave
Wanted to save my life, but you weren't there
Wanted to save my life, but you didn't care

Last night you grew fangs in my dreams
When I felt them, it was not as it seemed
Needed to save my life, but you weren't there

Bridge:
Chorus:

Untitled 38

Ignite this heart
Passion burns like fire
This love is ablaze
Burning up in your maze
This flame is my life

Chorus
Shooting star, farthest star
Shooting star, farthest star
Light up the night
Light up our lives
Weave wishes upon your lights

Sparkle in my soul
The feelings are strong
Glitter and glisten the sky
Capture the night
The flame feels so right

Chorus

Dead with You

I'm down and hurting now
And I'm trying so hard
To find what it's all about
And turn it inside out

Chorus :
    How I feel, is it a lie?
    And what I feel, is it a lie?
    Oh I'm tired of this life
    Lost and scared all the time
    But how I feel, is it a lie?
    And what I feel, is it a lie?

You think you're feeling
But you're asleep
A curse on your tongue
Berating me

I'm hanging on by these threads
That burn one at a time
I still breathe and smile
Hope to last one more mile

Bleeding eyes in clouds of fire
Drowns your life but takes you higher
I'm looking for my maker
Lightning, storms, clouds of vapor

I'm a wicked dream
That you pursue
A bullet in my gun
I'm dead with you

Other Writings & Excerpts From The Antiheroes: Treatise of a Lost Soul

The Void

I woke up this morning and crawled from my grave. I'm seeing the world through brand new eyes. I'm seeing life for the first time. I'm so alone. Only the courageous can abide the space inside this void. I hide. No one gets in, even when I want them, even when I want you. I'm an impetuous prince who needs no one's love or hate...or to love or hate, destroy or create. I keep to myself, not from human hands. Withdraw, then fire, not from human hands.

Time

Time closes in like a vice. Where did it all go? Those years when you never worried about the flow of time. Now you're rushing and running and racing the clock, trying to catch up with yesterday. Youth is a great pretender that deceives you. You'll never grow old when you're young, but now the track has played and your immortality was your own lie. Feeling spent, a time to cry. Mid-life crisis and a death sentence to boot. Remember when you were a king, ruling the roost?

Superhumans

I don't prefer or presume to be superhuman. What I write here is nothing more than my interpretation of personal observations, not based on any research or scientific evidence. I never aspired to write but feel compelled to do so, driven in large part by my profound feelings about being an outcast and its relevance to the concept of comparative human greatness versus the indifference that is becoming more and more the norm of the masses.

Great institutions are built on the ideals of great human beings. We need more greatness in people. We have become a lethargic, dumb society compared to earlier generations who didn't rely entirely on others such as the media, and in some cases the written word, to tell them what to think and how to think. Many nowadays have become enraged without knowing why. This is dangerous.

Greatness is an ideal based on observation of those around you. People who become great are able to unteach themselves the processes and expectations that every person is taught from birth. Most of us look but are unable to see. The superhuman has the ability to perceive even an everyday situation introspectively, to filter the unnecessary information and break it down to its basic premise. Superhumans don't think about their cognitive or intuitive processes. They just act intuitively upon their ideals.

Most great people are first seen as rebels, upstarts, disturbers of the peace, just plain weird or insane. "Norms" tend to need confirmation and acceptance. When it comes to recognition of human greatness, most people are arrogant in their mediocrity and "sameness," apprehensive about accepting someone's greatness until the herd and/or the media have said so. Only then is the superhuman accepted as one of "us." Only then are most people believers in the neighbor.

This may sound condescending toward the general populace, so some balance is offered in this discussion with myself. The dynamics between norms and superhumans is tenuous at best. Superhumans often do not get on well with "norms" because they have such divergent perspectives. The approach and the lifestyle of the superhuman causes alienation from the masses without desire or effort to appreciate or accommodate. In fact, the superhuman response is often contempt. The superhuman can tend to place too little value on the herd, and even on peers, with negative consequences. The island sinks.

So much greatness, so much superhumanity, is buried within the vast, overpowering mainstream noise, so much of it driven by realities created by corporate interests. Current realities will obscure great people and limit the greatness of institutions.

Art

Great art is created by the "abnormal" seeking enlightenment of the human spirit. To most people, great artists seem off-kilter because they are different or do not think like others. In another sense, the artist aspires to godliness with art being the pursuit of perfection....never to be achieved.

Art touches us not singularly, but as a whole. It lifts and refines civilization. One-on-one interactions with the artist are frequently not understood because the artist is thinking of the whole while the individual is looking for personal relevance. Many people look for personal entertainment, such as they would find in a book or in a movie, rather than greater purpose. Great art elevates human consciousness.

Integrity is the key ingredient. All great art has integrity.

Remorse
December 12, 2007

I realized something today that it seems has taken years to become clear. I couldn't say for sure the color of my ex-girlfriend's eyes and I spent 3 ½ years with her! I look but I don't see! I'm arrogant and self-absorbed and I've treated people who love me like shit! I never earned her love; I just expected it. I used her and took her for granted. No wonder she left me just like the one before her. It has taken several relationships for me to learn a valuable lesson. People are special and I am not superior to anyone. I've ruined a great thing 3 times over and it's too late in my life to keep making these stupid mistakes. All treated like shit and all turned on me. I hurt them and myself.....never again!

Punch Up the Quo
November 2007

Most people look at their current state and say, "This is who I am," but that's not who you are. That's who you were, tainted by residual thoughts and actions from your past. To look at your current state through the lens of the past is to define yourself in a fixed state and will doom you to a future of the same unless you shift your perspective. Visualize and you will materialize. Close your eyes and see it. Release it into the universe and trust that the universe will figure out how to manifest it.

Cruisin'

There's something about the way the wheel gently balances between my hands, and the feel of the driving gloves gives me security. The lines on the highway hypnotize and I stare as they rush past into infinity. These things focus my contemplation. I've loved music, but for the wrong reasons--not as art or a mode of communication, but a fucking pleasure cruise.

Rant on Censorship & Organized Religion

Here's a nation that preaches freedom: freedom of speech, freedom of religion. Here's a nation that condones violence in our entertainment: in our media, in our sports. A large number of male American youth ages 6 and up are skating through suburban streets beating each other with sticks, and we encourage this. It's exciting.

Yet some have the audacity to preach about the rightful content of a song. I don't hear you objecting about violence and sex in media and sports. What about their rightful content? I think someone should object to the imposition of your will on the artist. What makes you right? What makes you so high and mighty? You could reevaluate your priorities and use your energies for better purposes like poverty, crime, cruelty, hunger and environmental issues.

You are the culprits, preachers and censors. You're as Great Britain once was to New England.

Stomp your boot til your foot is black and blue
Not everyone will be like you
Yell and scream and pound your book
You disclude everywhere you fucking look
Disclude, exclude, segregate everywhere you march your boot

Organized religion
Like organized crime
Point your finger
Religious blind

You'd hold for ransom if you could bind
The weak and gullible to your behind
You spin and twist truths to get your way
To meet your goal on donation day

Where does freedom hide its beat-up head?
Assimilation on the hunt, can't let it win.

The following excerpts are from The Antiheroes: Treatise of a Lost Soul. **They are stream of consciousness, self-talk, of the main character Fade.**

Artwork by Ryan Sulfaro

"God, why is this happening to me?"
God's response: "It has nothing to do with me. You fuckers are on your own down there."

Photo by Jess Allera

What is it that keeps me here I sometimes wonder... Maybe I'm biased because Detroit is all I've ever known. I had an opportunity to travel briefly when I was younger and have been to a few other cities, but I didn't care for them as I do Detroit. I don't know why exactly unless it's because of the history and hard-edged reputation of this city. Call me crazy...or perhaps it's as close to spiritualism as I ever get...but I can feel the life force of this city emanating from its buildings and oozing up from its streets. I can't fathom living anywhere else...

You have to know this city intimately to appreciate it. It's the dark secrets and hidden places that make Detroit so special, places like the tiny Comet Bar where the atmosphere is warm and inviting to all elements of the street. Here you might find a down-and-out hooker-addict serving drinks or a homeless alcoholic sitting at the bar. I fondly recall an evening when the Comet was hosting karaoke. Three young people who were living in an abandoned factory were there with their two dogs, and one of the girls took the stage to sing accompanied by one of the dogs, a white pit, that laid at her feet while she sang. The dog had eyebrows that had been drawn on with eyebrow pencil or felt marker. One of the three told me their dogs always come first, that they feed the dogs when there isn't enough food to go around. These are the places, people and circumstances that only a native Detroiter or seasoned denizen would know, and this knowing makes you belong or not belong here. To most people, Motown isn't pretty to look at, ravaged by blight and misuse, but for who I am and what I am, I can think of no other place that could so readily accommodate me and my friends. There's beauty in the ruins and the 'urbanart' of Spiderman-like climbers who spray-paint rooftop 'tags,' graffiti that can be seen from great distances on towering abandoned buildings. I admire the climber-artists who are actually daring stunt men, thrill seekers, rebels with and without a cause, and prophets all at the same time.

I love this city, but it's a love tempered by caution and respect for danger. I'm here and I'm here forever. I rarely leave the confines of the city and haven't done so in years. I will die here. **I live and play in my own graveyard**. Time is slipping away from me and my friends and our days are numbered. We've been too lucky to continue our streak of fortune much longer. Something has to give eventually, and that will be our lives.... Who really wants to live forever? Maybe I do, or maybe I just can't grasp what that really means. Most likely death will become preferable at some point, so I don't worry about it and will welcome it when it comes.

Dark. It's always so dark here, but I feel safe within the confines of the loft. My nightlight and the lights from the vanity in the bathroom provide the only illumination tonight in this seemingly cavernous space where I reside. This loft seems so big and overly empty at night, a constant reminder that I have nothing really to speak of, just a dark, empty, dusty space...but I think I like it this way. Yes, I definitely like it this way. No connections, affiliations or responsibilities. No invisible chains to restrain me. I don't need much. I never need much come to think of it. Just the bare essentials: alcohol, drugs, music, makeup, girls, in that order, and sometimes...food. Having nothing is easy and free, and since I have relatively little, I think I'm qualified to comment on the subject of the much underrated concept of simplicity. Keeping things simple makes me jubilant and giddy with a heightened sense of unfettered freedom seldom known to the general populace, an existence reflected by my humble domicile.

I've learned so much from my girlfriends, how to make clothes and how to dye my hair and apply makeup. These are important skills for me.... Girls also seem to have impeccable taste in music, an instinctive sixth sense about what is good and true art. Much of what I listen to is from my girlfriends. I can't give them enough praise regarding these things, beauty and music and art....This passion for dressing up is a large part of what I admire about the Goth subculture and what makes it unique. I think it stems from the creative and intelligent people it attracts....You become living, breathing art....It is a celebration of life in which we immerse ourselves without fear of death. Death is a part of life and Goths embrace it, hence the primary color we wear is black. But this is no funeral; we are here to celebrate and express ourselves to the fullest extent possible, so some dress in extremes, making the Goth existence dynamic and always interersting. I am proud to be a part of this scene. I was born for it. I want to suck the marrow out of life and the Goth subculture is the bone...I dress for an androgenous look. Goth males aspire to the male-female persona. Being in touch with your feminine side is a sensibility not possessed by many males. It takes a confident man to do it well and make it his own without losing touch with who he truly is. Most people will instinctively understand if it's a true expression of your character and not pretense for the sake of show. If it's genuine, comfortably appreciative of the feminine, it's the mark of beauty. A true Goth male takes the subculture and its way of life seriously. Androgyny can be very cool if done well and from the heart.

Artwork by Ryan Sulfaro

We're renegades looking for our place on an unforgiving, merciless landscape. If I were an animal totem spirit, I would be a black rabbit. I **always** wait for his call. Death is a constant companion for us all, and I have The Black Rabbit tattooed on my right side. When The Black Rabbit calls, you must go. [Refers to the Black Rabbit of Inle' in Watership Down by Richard Adams]

This may sound trite, but we all are influenced by popular culture in one way or another. I'm no exception. We all need a belief or ideology and we all lean toward some dogma or ethos that has presented itself to us, be it religion, culture, creed, science or philosophy. These are the things that guide our perceptions, interpretations, and responses to our world and to situations confronting us. Who's to say that a movie, an animation, a book, a play, a sculpture or a painting that moves you is any less credible a driver of one's perspective and belief system than a religion? They can all be significant and life changing. Religions are just man-made philosophies. Some people live by the tenets of a religion and others by the principles or message in a movie or a novel. It's all the same shit to me…to each their own…live and let live, unless someone deserves to die or must die for my survival, I guess.

I wonder what it is that I believe and how I would answer if I were forced to deal with the question of whether I believe in God. I know for sure that I'm not religious in the traditional sense. I don't like religion. It's man-made. Whatever man has created has flaws in abundance, and I don't like the way religions exclude and harshly judge those who don't agree with them and abide by their beliefs. I thought religions like Christianity were supposed to be all-inclusive and accepting of others, but I haven't seen much tolerance. On the contrary, it seems to me that most religions are exclusive. They tend to point their fingers at others who live or think differently, outside their particular dogma, and so they push people away and ridicule them.

And what about a higher power? Is there something out there that makes it all tick, some force that created the universe and moves all the pieces around? I don't believe in a Bible version of God or that man was made in God's image. Whatever the life force is, it's omnipotent, but I don't think it takes an active part in the lives of individual human beings. I believe it set life into motion and then just let it roll...for better or worse. I guess this makes me spiritual in a sense, and calling this presence "God" is fine for a lack of a better word. I think people are able to tap into spiritual energy in good and bad ways and through many means, most commonly prayer or meditation, and that this energy can sometimes intervene, or at least boost morale and spiritual strength enough to guide us in times of need...or destroy us if it's abused or used for evil purposes. I believe in something, but I'm not sure what that something is outside of this explanation.

It seems the primary difference between animals and human beings who interact within a pack hierarchy is that humans assert themselves in a number of different ways: strength of personality, intelligence, communicating to influence, aesthetics, money, or position. Animals, on the other hand, assert themselves through strength, size, and brute force, somewhat resembling my small group of friends except that it has never come to physical blows between us, even though we are feral at times.

I like to strive to be more like an animal because animals are the best living examples of perfection. We don't compare to their beauty and grace. What are we in comparison to the beauty and grace of a tiger or an eagle? They are always perfect in form. Every tiger is beautiful. They don't vary in form. Not so with humans. Some people are too tall, some too short. Some people are too fat, too skinny, etc. The list of less than attractive imperfections is lengthy with humans. Is there an ideal human form? If so, what percentage of the population would fit into that category? Very few if any. Our flaws are endless, and that's just in "looks" department. We hide our bodies in clothing and makeup to even be pleasing to ourselves. This is remarkable to me.

Animals in their natural environment don't act out of emotion or reason. They don't kill because they're angry or jealous. They don't harm out of malice or contempt. They are the perfect embodiment of nature, untarnished by the trivial feelings and motives that drive humans to all sorts of horrible actions. I love the simplicity and purity of what humans erroneously refer to as lower forms of life. They do what needs to be done for survival or self-preservation, never out of hatred or selfish love. They don't need concepts like good or evil to guide them. They just **are**.

The unbelievable human arrogance gets to me the most. We kill without compunction or impunity when something or someone is perceived as different, not one of "us." Why is this? All life has value, and all living things deserve the right to a life however insignificant we may think they are. We are the great arbiters who determine who and what can live and who and what should die, even in the wild where we pass judgment on the worth and right to life of certain species of animals such as wolves and coyotes. We didn't create life; we are merely part of it. You'd think with our higher intellect and "advanced" culture we'd be the great caretakers of life, not the judge and jury who decide the fate of all life on Earth. But instead of nurturing Earth and its creatures and taking what we need in a way that preserves, we destroy it and strip it of all resources, mostly out of greed, and give very little back.

It sickens me to no end how fucking overly important we think we are, especially on an individual basis, everyone out there running around doing their daily business thinking the fucking world revolves around them and their schedules. Everyone else is just in their way, slowing them down, and their business is way more important than anyone else's. It's all bullshit.

People think they're so fucking important and they're not. Everyone is replaceable, and each one of us is just a fucking number. Billions of fucking numbers that add up to shit. Each person is just a grain of sand on a beach, living in our own little bubbles of self-delusion about our personal importance. Life will always go on without you no matter who you are and how important you think you are. The only ones who really give a shit about you are yourself and your immediate family—however you define that term. No one else really gives a fuck about you, and why should they? That's part of the great design. Life goes on. There's perpetually the next link in the chain. It makes perfect sense to me. So why all the fucking arrogance?

Another thing I've noticed that goads me, and also has to do with people thinking they're overly important, is that no one listens. No one really likes to listen to anything. You know why? They're too fucking busy talking. People are in love with talking about nothing! They either love to hear themselves talk for the sake of making noise, or they're so pathetically lonesome and insecure that they need to babble on about nothing. Again, it's the delusion of self-importance, or in some cases a pitiful need for acceptance, the incessant talking about nothing that really matters to anyone except the person who's talking and talking and talking and talking. People entertain themselves this way or try to keep themselves company even when they're in the company of others. It's inane. They talk all day long and don't say a fucking thing that's worth saying. I wish people would talk less but say more and cut out all the bullshit. Then maybe someone would listen. Get to the fucking point already then shut the fuck up and listen for a response that makes sense. Talking is a symptom of people's mostly unimportant wants and needs, not necessities but trivialities, things that just don't matter, things that create confusion and unnecessary drama. Fuck these people who talk meaninglessly and don't even seem to realize it. They don't hear themselves and how stupid they sound. They should be recorded and then made to sit in a room they can't escape from and listen to a tape of themselves talking played at high volume. Maybe then they would understand how fucking annoying they are. I'm quiet. If I don't have something worthwhile to say, I just don't. The world would be a better place if people would learn to listen more and talk less.

While I'm on a rant, there's the English language. What a stupid fucking language. We have too many words that mean the same thing. Animals say more in a look to one another than a small pamphlet of our stupid, overbearing litanies. Most of what most people have to say is just fucking empty rhetoric, anyway. Fucking senseless and useless, lots of empty words. That's a problem I have lately, trying to decipher all the shit talk that comes at me. I've created a mental filter that tunes it all out. I either ignore people or let their words hit a barrier just inside my ears, a wall that bounces all their words right back out. I can even do this while holding a conversation with them and smiling at them as they babble on about nothing, and I nod as if I'm taking it all in when I'm really not processing a word they say.

What is this I'm feeling? What are these emotions that are pulling my logic and understanding of myself in directions I don't want to go? I've never let myself fall into the position of caring for anyone. Never let myself? Or I just don't know how? I was never shown how. Maybe I'm not capable of that human and most powerful emotion called love. I know I've never been loved, not as a child or as an adult. I like what I'm feeling for Niv, and it scares me more than any street fight. She seems to actually care for me and understand me. I feel horrible and frightened. There's only so much I can tell her about myself before she'll have to leave me. She's not like the other girls. She's a true giver and would put my needs above her own even when she's the one who needs help. She's the most unselfish person I've ever met and why she has chosen me is beyond my grasp. I've been somewhat ambivalent toward her. I'm at a loss about her, and I'm not sure how I'll handle this. She's a huge risk for me. It's always fucking about me and I hate that about myself, but that's all there is. That's all I know. Bringing her into my world could hurt both of us, could kill both of us. Maybe somehow, if I'm able to see this through, she could be a way out for me just as she seems to think I'm a way out for her? This could turn everything around and she could become my savior. How fucking romantic. Ha! We could save each other. My cynicism never abates. I don't trust myself.

I think being a member of the human race comes with a huge responsibility that many can't seem to uphold. We have to be constantly reminded what human existence ideally entails, often through the insights and reflections of authors and artists who move our spirits and souls positively forward, seeking continuous improvement and enlightenment. I find it disappointing that humanism has to be taught to us, and then we have to work at attaining it. It should at least be intuitive, although it could be argued that it is intrinsic but frequently cast aside in the interest of personal desires and ulterior motives. I believe we just aren't pure enough, that we aren't instinct-driven enough, like animals, knowing how to be who we are and what to do with our "superior" intellects. A cat doesn't need to learn how to be a cat. It just **is** a cat.

A human being needs to be taught and guided more than other living creatures. How ironic is that for the most intelligent creature on Earth? We arrive here like blind and dumb aliens and stumble about aimlessly and without purpose if we aren't shown how to live and let live…or convinced it's a greater good to do so. Even when we're shown, many of us are still unable or unwilling to evolve in an upward direction. People mostly lack appreciation of the great responsibility we have as the caretakers of the world and all that's in it. Most don't care anyway. We're hedonists, fixated on personal desires.

Among multitudes of others, I've been a consummate failure at evolving into a good human being. Maybe it's not completely our fault, but personal responsibility for one's actions should be paramount. Everyone wants to pass the buck, even in the direction of a god. We need scapegoats, but that being written here, there are social and economic conditions that can lead one to extreme measures in order to survive. That, I think, is the major cause of disharmony in the world and the catalyst for most aggressive behaviors. Human backlash against human-created social and political injustice and inequities is perpetual, ever flowing from the human spirit and the need to survive.

Brutal reality yields aftermath that will always be, like the by-products and waste from any system, whether it's a social-political structure, a motor, a factory, a family or a single living organism. Society is a big machine that produces, in an over-simplified sense, good people and damaged people, damaged people being the waste and by-products, failures of the system. The machine will run you over if you don't meet its demands, and then it'll break you down to a creature who is merely the sum of your cells, a broken spirit in a futile existence. Once you're expunged from the system, it's hard to re-enter, especially once you've done what you had to do…once you've become a waste product of the machine called society. What's left then? Faith? Hope? God? Death? Always Death, the only certainty in life.

I like to pretend to see and feel through the eyes and emotions of Vader (Fade's dog in The Antiheroes). I'd like to think this helps me to better perceive and understand all aspects of life. The more I understand the perfect creatures, animals, and especially dogs, the more I also understand what it should mean to be human. The more I understand, the more I hate people and the deplorable way they treat living things including the way they treat each other. Man's inhumanity to man reaches back across the ages. The arrogance intertwined with ignorance is beyond belief for me. We're a vicious race that is so unpredictable…no rhyme, no reason. Animals are predictable. They act in a reasonable and just manner that corresponds with, and is warranted by, the situation. They act based on their natural instincts for survival and their past experiences. A human being, on the other hand, is capable of great compassion when it's convenient, followed by great cruelty if it serves a whim or a motive. We are truly creatures of opposite extremes and unpredictability no matter what the situation. We're subversive and untrustworthy and demonstrate erratic behaviors that astound and injure others at every turn. We are the only creatures who commit genocide, torture, and suicide. Every animal has an innate instinct to do whatever is necessary to protect its life and survive. Life is precious to animals. We, on the other hand, kill each other and ourselves every day. To humankind, life is cheap, and even while we pretend it's paramount, that's really just a civilized façade. We love death, as long as it's someone else's death, and violence. We are truly blight and a disgrace—a cosmic joke, a fabulous disaster—the means to our own end.

I think insanity is not knowing the difference between fiction and reality, living inside an illusion you've created in your head that you act on as if it's reality. It stands to reason, then, that you wouldn't be aware that you're crazy because your illusion has become your reality. When you interact with the reality that is perceived by others, depending on how off kilter your version of reality is compared with theirs, you are deemed crazy to that extent. But isn't everyone's version of reality real? Doesn't everyone perceive things differently? If so, then how can anyone truly be crazy? Or, maybe everyone is crazy. Maybe the people who are considered insane are actually the ones catching a glimpse of sanity and the true reality? This drives me crazy just thinking about it.

Even so, I have to wonder if I'm insane. Metal (a character in The Antiheroes) thinks he's Elton John and gets locked up, but my freaky friends and I are the ones going around killing people! Who's crazier? Metal or the rest of us? I wonder, if we ever get caught, could we get off with an insanity plea? Would a jury think we're all nuts? Why not? We look it and act it. Maybe we are crazy and we don't know it because of the off-center reality we know and live, the only reality we know and live, like Metal when he became Elton John. For us, maybe it's perpetual and never ending.

Maybe I've never been sane, ever. I don't feel crazy, but how would I know? This is kind of scary for me to think about, wondering about my life, not really knowing or understanding whether I'm actually a madman. I guess I'm capable of anything if I'm capable of murder! What's not off limits for me? Nothing when it comes to human beings because I hate them unless they're children. That's crazy, isn't it? Perhaps the difference between Metal and me is that he is disconnected and I'm not...I just don't care. Seems like a person who does what I do might be called a sociopath? I might tend to believe that except that I often feel empathy, pity and compassion as well as moral responsibility...but again, mostly for children and animals.

Sometimes a sudden, unexplainable gloom casts a shadow over me without apparent cause or warning, like a dark pall that obscures all other thoughts except those it brings unbidden into my mind. It defies all logic and reason. I feel the weight of all suffering and cruelty in the world bearing down upon me, the destruction and devastation wrought by mankind throughout the ages. It seems the human race is an infestation, spreading steadily like a disease until the earth is now on the brink of decay and death. When this happens, I'm forced to stop whatever I'm doing to deal with these thoughts and I find myself on the verge of tears. These heavy thoughts leave me as quickly as they come, but they always leave me knowing I'm powerless to undo or prevent what comes next in the saga of humankind and thinking of a quote from the character played by Marlon Brando at the end of the movie Apocalypse Now, as he holds his head in his hands and whispers, "The horror. The horror."

Most people don't act on impulse. If they did, the world would be unoccupied by humans. Most people fear the consequences that are imposed by society. Sane people are deemed sane because they're able to function within an acceptable range of behaviors that are based on perceptions, the common experience of the majority. This has been called consensus reality. Most comply and mind their steps to avoid the consequences. In other words, they reign in their impulses out of fear. Everyone has the capacity, under certain circumstances, to kill when our primal "animal" instincts kick in. Laws and consequences will never change that. Then there are people who kill, not for immediate survival, but because a line is crossed in their minds, a line that has slowly developed during one's lifetime. These people kill without remorse like it's a job.

That's me. That's why Spam is saner than I am. I'm more scared of being caught than anything. That's the point. When you can kill because of something like spite, without an immediate threat to your own survival, you've stepped over the line into what I think qualifies as insanity. I'm there.

By mainstream social and mental health standards, the people in the diner were innocent, yet I took their lives and led my friends to do the same…except for Spam who didn't kill any of them, but now he's guilty by association. I've become my own greatest threat to continued freedom and brought us all to ruin through my recklessness and cold, detached violence. I've become intolerant, a trait I've always hated in others. The only difference is that I don't publicly ridicule others until I've been pushed into a ruthless, vengeful frenzy and feel compelled to show them the error of their ways, to brutally teach them tolerance and civility. Irony again. I guess I'm too sensitive for a crass and cruel society that feels to so many like it's based on exclusion. It offends my sense of justice. Be **this** or be cast out, or in the case of organized religion, another **social institution** presented as the word of God, be shunned…but I digress.

Maybe I've become too insecure, to the point of judging others as I've always been judged. Do unto others what has been done unto you. I've taken this sentiment to the extreme. Society won't tolerate people like me who make our own rules and step outside the law, and maybe it shouldn't. Yes, it shouldn't. I'm in the wrong and I don't care, but if I know the difference between right and wrong, does that perhaps make me sane?

Here I go again, on a rant about the infestation of the planet by human beings. And on top of the obvious trouble caused by sheer numbers of mostly worthless people, their overbearing arrogance is intolerable. The over-exaggerated importance we place on ourselves is a sickening farce that manifests itself at the expense of all life forms around us. Egocentrism is rampant. Look at the media, television being the worst. Everyone on TV is made up to look perfect. The media's widespread influence has resulted in the pompous and the vain becoming the standard aspired to by everyday people. Celebrities made to be gods. It's all a lie. It's been that way since the advent of civilization, man valuing himself above all other life forms and some men placing themselves above other human beings. Look at the Romans and the Egyptians, emperors being revered as living gods on earth with unlimited power over the life and death of all others around them, or rather beneath them. People by the thousands died at their whim.

We're eating away at our own feet, and we will fall. You can decide whether that statement pertains to human social dysfunction or to me and my friends...or both. A just fate befalls all who believe they walk on a plane above others, including other life forms, who act as judge and jury. A just fate will also visit extreme outliers like us who dare to commit the ultimate transgression.

I don't think most people truly understand the need to be alone. A lot of people say they do, but that's just talk. Most people live with someone: family, friends, a roommate, a significant other. People are pack creatures by nature and aren't good at being alone. Those who live alone usually seek to change that situation. This is why most people don't get to know themselves very well, because they're constantly getting feedback from others about every move they make and everything they do and even how they think. The only way to truly get to know yourself is through isolation and introspection without interference from others, coming to terms with all your demons and understanding what makes you tick as a person. I think one has to live alone for at least three years to accomplish this. Only then can you realize who you are and recognize your flaws without trying to make excuses for them or justify them like most people do. They rationalize that they acted a certain way because of this or that, or someone made them do this or that because of something that person said or did. That's such bullshit. Most people won't fully accept responsibility for their actions because they're weak and insecure about who they think they might be…and underlying all that, it's because they just don't know who the fuck they really are. They're confused and stumble through life in a maze, letting shit happen however it happens…as long as no shit sticks to them. Many jump into anything at the drop of a hat—love, marriage, business or whatever and then end up fucked up and sometimes paying for it, along with others, for the rest of their lives.

I don't know anyone who has really been alone for any significant period of time except me. All my friends live with someone. I've lived alone for as long as I can remember. It was hard to come to terms with this at a couple points in my life, but I understand it and accept it now. I've come to actually need my aloneness and couldn't live with another person. It would interrupt my thoughts. I think it was Morrissey who said that it's a luxury to live by oneself. I believe it is. Most people, however, would not be able to live alone simply because they need frequent external input. Me, I love the absence of intrusion into my inner world, but it is difficult in some ways. Physical needs are an obvious challenge but can be attended to without being in an ongoing close relationship, the lack of which leads to an emotional void for some. But for me, love has never been a priority. I'm not sure why.

A void I do wish could be filled is one that requires some spiritual presence, 'God' most would say. I could never identify with any religion and maintain any spiritual integrity, but it would be fulfilling to believe in something worthwhile and meaningful outside of myself. I don't know how to accomplish this. I've prayed before, but I feel like a hypocrite doing so for a few reasons. I don't know what to say, first of all, and if I ask for help, it feels like the only time I talk to God is when I need something or I'm in trouble. Also, I think I'm really confused deep down. That being said, I'd much prefer confusion and unresolved doubts to having clear, undaunted faith in the misguided and harmful ideologies that are out there.

I'm not sure if I believe in God. It seems the God concept is believed by most others, but I have doubts that God would listen to me anyway which makes praying feel useless for me. I want to believe in something in my own way…but I don't know how or if it's even possible for me. It is often said that one has to either believe wholeheartedly or not at all, that there can't be any uncertainty. My ambivalence is what stands between me and spiritual enlightenment, any relationship with a higher power.

Ambivalence and cynicism also keep me safely away from false prophets and preachers who believe they are qualified to interpret and deliver the word of the higher power. Once a long time ago, a girlfriend's mom told me that I'll go to hell because I was never baptized. This is the kind of religious shit that turns me off and alienates many potential followers, people who are looking for some deeper meaning to their existence. It's religion gone wrong. Believe as I do or else. This seems to be a common thread with all of the religions I've encountered.

Religion should be all inclusive, not exclusive. Religion's followers often point fingers and exclude people who are not of the same belief. More than half of the world's people are followers of religions other than Christianity and Catholicism. Does that mean all of those millions upon millions of people are misguided, just wrong, or going to some version of hell? What a crock of shit the Christians and Catholics have been brewing and selling to the masses over the centuries. I'm sure other religions are just as bad, so I'll include all of them, some who kill each other because of religious intolerance and even kill their own when they step outside the teachings. Western religions haven't cornered the market on narrow-minded ideological propaganda. What total fucking arrogance to think that any religion delivers the truth about God and life hereafter.

So we're back to human arrogance, and we're all full of it. Americans have the audacity to think God favors this country and its people above all other nations and peoples. That's fucking stupid and naïve to say the least. We always believe God is on our side. How arrogant is that? I don't think a God worthy of the position would be on any nation's side. They say God's chosen people are in Israel, but they forget that Jesus, the great philosopher and teacher, was actually just a Jew gone bad, an outcast in his time among his own people and others because of the same problems we still have with religion…and with religious people…that I'm writing about.

It seems to me that even though some churches try to include everyone and minimize intolerance, so many others past and present have done such large-scale damage that they're all now facing backlash from people who aren't just mindless sheep.

The best I can say in a prayer, when I can find the right words, is "Help me move forward." I'm such a consistent sinner that I feel I'll never be accepted and furthermore that I'm not doing the right things to have faith in myself much less in any higher power. I wonder if I can continue doing what I do, as it's all I know and all I have, and still somehow fill the spiritual void inside myself and attain some level of contentment. Sometimes at night I need to talk to someone, so I talk to a God who may or may not exist. Whether God listens to me, who can know? I tell God the truth, though. I'm lost and I'm sorry. I wonder if a real God would forsake me...or forgive me?

———•———

Hopefully without sounding sarcastic or naïve, the founders of this nation had it right when the Second Continental Congress expressed in writing, in the Declaration of Independence, the premises upon which this republic would carry forth. Every person has the right to the pursuit of happiness, **pursuit** being the key word. Happiness, however, has to be chased after again and again, pursued most diligently, like trying to catch something that is elusive, moving fast and changing shape as it travels. Everyone has the right to pursue happiness, but that doesn't mean you'll ever grab it or be able to hold onto it. This is so ironic because happiness seems like a simple concept when you think about it. It's usually easy enough to smile and laugh, outward behaviors that are so often associated with happiness. Even the sound of the word happiness seems relaxed and easy and smooth. Some people seem to think you can take happiness for granted as if it's a natural state, but the hard truth is that personal happiness is extremely evasive. There is no greater intangible in life, much more difficult to attain than money, success, or even love. I would choose happiness over anything if I could somehow pin it down and keep it. What might be described as happiness by one person is not the same for others. It wears many different coats. For me happiness has always been driven by freedom. I don't think I know anyone who is truly free or happy. We all merely continue the **pursuit**.

Another concept I often think about is this: If you had to sum up life in just one word, what word would best describe it? I think the answer to this question isn't as variable as what makes one happy. There is one word that best describes life. I'm sure this would be argued by some, but I'm convinced of it. The word is **irony**. Nothing ever turns out the way you want it to or think it will. Even the smallest things are subject to this rule of the universe. Do you ever drop something and can't find it or need something and can't find it, but when you're not looking for it, it turns up? People spend their lives dreaming of becoming something like a rock star or an actor or an athlete but end up doing something completely different like becoming an accountant or a doctor. Then there are those who never aspire to be musicians or actors, yet they somehow find themselves immersed in those arts and achieve great success. Many people who desire fame never attain it, perhaps because their tiring pursuit and lust for it cause strained or contrived efforts, while others who don't struggle just fall into it. Many people who pursue money never acquire it while others who don't even think about it become rich. Life and the **pursuit** of happiness often take opposite directions it seems. There are anomalies and exceptions, but this is how things work out most of the time. Life happens while you're making other plans, as observed by John Lennon. Life is irony.

Sometimes I'm overcome with an almost unbearable sadness. It comes from nowhere and can flatten me into a lethargic state. Thoughts about man's inhumanity to man and his cruelty to lesser, or in my opinion more perfect , life forms that we dominate through dastardly human intellect and reason, can be triggered without a catalyst. My profound sadness can stem from past visions out of movies or happenings heard on the news or read in a book, and they have the power to send me into a state of severe depression bordering on anguish. It feels as if the weight of these crimes falls upon my shoulders along with the rest of humanity, like I'm responsible for atrocities that have nothing whatsoever to do with me.

Some of the cruelty is so hideous that I believe it sends off a very powerful wave of negativity, some far-reaching frequency that strikes me along with the universe. Because of my inclination toward gentle spirits like the Goths, I know that the weighty karma of inhumane acts past and present strikes others in the same way it strikes me. Some acts are simply evil, done for the sake of being cruel and malicious, and should not be tolerated by the world. Malevolent events make themselves cosmically known, like a snapshot or impression in time, like a ghost or a restless spirit who has died under extreme injustice. These spiritual shock waves strike me unexpectedly and are almost unbearable. It's very difficult to fend them off.

The history of mankind is filled with war and its countless atrocities. They make me hate mankind with a renewed passion. Our species has always been barbaric and not much has changed except that technology has improved our precision and expanded our capabilities. Spiritual and ethical evolution have not kept pace with technological advances.

The cruelties that shake me hardest are those committed against animals. There are the news stories about animal abuse by individuals, but then there's broader scale abuse that sends veritable shock waves across the universe. Look at China's fur trade, the practice of skinning animals alive. Call it a cultural difference if you wish but it's indefensible–evil incarnate. All you soul-less fucks who have done this type of shit will get what's coming to you wherever you are. Karma is a mother fucker, and everyone gets what they deserve no matter how long it takes. You will eventually pay and suffer, perhaps not even half of what you deserve, but you will suffer.

All this probably sounds hypocritical and contradictory coming from a man who has himself taken life, and maybe it is. I could try to justify the killing I've done by saying it has been in self-defense or that those who were killed deserved it somehow, but I won't try at this point. I don't presume to know what's right or wrong anymore. But I do know there's a difference between what I've done and core-level evil, and whether I'm right or wrong, that's what I believe in my heart. I know I'm not an evil person, if I know anything at all. I'm as lost as everyone else it seems, even moreso. I can only reflect on these things with hope for some consolation, understanding, or therapy for myself. Forgiveness? Absolution? Recompense? Do those even exist for me?

The holidays make one realize how fucked up and out of control the human race really is. For one thing, the season gives you a glimpse of the massive numbers of people out there. How much longer can the earth sustain a population of ravagers? Take. Take. Take. Take. Take. Kill. Kill. Kill. Kill. Kill. Kill. Consume. Consume. Consume. Consume. Waste. Waste. Waste. Waste. Waste. What are we giving back so that the planet is able to sustain itself? Can a damaging, pervasive species such as us continue? I strongly believe we need a selective breeding program. People who would make good parents often don't have children, and people who breed like rats produce rat-like offspring who have unfortunately become the status quo. No wonder the world is populated with so many assholes, idiots and mindless followers. If you don't believe it, watch some reality TV and ask yourself why millions tune in.

It's scary to see people shopping at Christmas. It scares the shit out of me.

Detroit, sometime in the early nineties. It's around October, my favorite time of year—dark, damp and gray, a perpetual overcast that goes on day in and day out. Depressing really, I would imagine for most, but I'm used to it. For me it's home.

It's evening and the skyline is lit with a tinge of dull orange and metallic blue from "the fire in the sky." That's what I call it. One can see it clearly from the River Rouge overpass, really a bridge, when driving over it into the city, especially approaching from the south. Open flames spew from high towers, burning continuously day and night like the bonfire of some weird cult. I love the fire in the sky. It makes me smile for some strange reason. I'm not exactly sure why, but I feel comforted by it. I'm home, the place where I belong. When the fires aren't burning, I feel something is wrong and it disrupts my sense of security.

Most people would want this burning to stop as it's probably filled with industrial toxins. No, it's definitely pollution pouring into the open sky, releasing fumes from the steel mills and oil refineries and exhaust from plant furnaces to produce the horrible sulfur-like stench in the area surrounding the bridge, but I like it. Not so much the smell, but the fire that is Detroit. It's so fitting here, a monumental symbol of what made the Motor City great, an industrial throwback, a reminder of Detroit's glory days with the fires of industry still meekly burning like the weak pulse of a giant failing heart. The fire in the sky alerts me like a flashing warning sign, reminding me, as it should remind others coming into the city, of where they are.

There are a few places where I like to hang out—small, crusty dive bars. Real life seems more in focus for me at these places. They touch the day-to-day struggle of most people. Just as City Club (Detroit's Goth-Industrial night club) is for more youthful social outcasts, the dives are for the older outcasts. I feel at home in these places. I like their quiet and their musty ambiance, where there are few people and everyone minds their own business. These are the haunts of other lost souls and the downtrodden whose dreams have been broken. No one pretends to be anyone they are not. No pretenses or bravado here, just real life. The truth is found in these places, the warty truth, and you have to face it like a mirror in the morning along with the pungent smells of decay, urine, and mildew in the carpets, the hazy air and dim lights that cast shadows on smoke-stained walls and ceilings and old pictures in cracked frames. Nothing is perfect or too clean, just barely clean enough for practical use and sometimes not. The gritty dives are the bare naked soul of the city, the unscrubbed reality, heart-beating true to life. I am here.

Temple Bar on Cass Avenue,
one of Abe's (Fade's) favorite bars.

On the porch at 322

Of Dragons and Music: 2010-2014

Drawing by Abe, early teen years

If there was one consistent pattern to Abe's love of music and his choices of literature, it was diversity. His collection of recordings includes symphonies, operas, pop, rock, heavy metal, jazz, Frank Sinatra, Tony Bennett, Jeff Buckley and Patsy Cline. His relationship with Detroit and the many musicians, artists and colorful characters whose lives touched his became more apparent than ever when family and friends shared the heart-wrenching job of gathering Abe's belongings at his beloved "322," the house where he grew up, and in the loft where he lived over the Nuclear Lounge. There were times when we were overcome by sorrow and times when we broke into laughter as memories were triggered by Abe's writings, music and other items. His most prized possessions, his books, include fantasy novels by Michael Moorcock, J.R.R. Tolkien, R.A. Salvatore, Anne Rice, Hideyuki Kikuchi and Aleister Crowley alongside Shakespeare and books on philosophy. Perpetually the dungeon master, he had amassed a large collection of unopened (in plastic) Dungeons & Dragons publications. His clothing and boots reflect his affinity with the Goth subculture and his hard-driving metal / glam stage persona. Many T-shirts are reminders of Abe's music favorites, off-color sense of humor and peaceful disposition: Kansas, Ramones, MotorHead, "Sorry, mom, your kid is fucked up," "You're all whores" and a hooded Marvin Gaye sweatshirt bearing a song quote "War is not the answer."

In the years following Champion Eternal, his immersion in Detroit's Gothic / Emo subculture and performances with Slave to the Beautiful, Abe wrote *The Antiheroes* and was tied to daily operations at The Nuclear Lounge, the bar he owned in downriver Detroit (Newport) where he lived in a small loft during his last two years. Never existing more than a heartbeat away from live music, those years occasionally found Abe performing with bands such as Baby Face Finster (Abe Succoro [Sulfaro], lead and back-up vocals and rhythm guitar; Scott Mroz, lead guitar; Jason Cossin, drums and back-up vocals; Mike Berry, bass guitar, lead and back-up vocals) and Bad Dog USA (Bob Tremblay, rhythm guitar; Jerry Kuck, bass guitar; Abe Sulfaro, vocals; Jeff Hall, drums; Bill Bouvier, lead guitar). It was Bob Tremblay, a retired Detroit police officer, who provided some of the insider glimpses of crime and law enforcement that Abe wrote about in The Antiheroes. Bob was present at the Nuclear Lounge and respectfully closed the bar when they received the call about Abe's passing.

Abe performing with Baby Face Finster

Bad Dog USA on stage at the Nuclear Lounge.
Left to right: Bob Tremblay, Jerry Kuck, Abe, Jeff Hall, Bill Bouvier

Memories From Family & Friends

This section was added to Memoirs late in its compilation. Recollections flowed forth during interactions with Abe's friends, now extended family. Other stories were shared at two gatherings in his memory, one at Reflections Bar & Grille in southwest Detroit and one at the Diamond back Saloon near Ann Arbor. His Aunt Royetta placed a quote at the front of the memory book: "Sometimes memories sneak out of my eyes and roll down my cheeks." (Unknown Author)

Abe as Best Man

Dayve (Watson) Disintegration, a character in The Antiheroes and real-life friend, recalls meeting Abe at a martini bar in Detroit. Dayve was wearing make-up in Goth fashion and began to cry, telling Abe about his heartache over a girl who had broken up with him.

Abe: "Go cry to your mom. That's what moms are for. When I get upset, I call my mother. I don't bother my friends with it. Friends help me enjoy life."

Abe bought Dayve a shot and handed him a cocktail napkin. "Here, dry your eyes. Your eyeliner is running. Man the fuck up, you sappy bastard."

———•———

Once upon an evening on a crowded People Mover in downtown Detroit, a very impaired woman was making loud, obnoxious comments to everyone around her. She was obviously looking for trouble, and she happened to be standing next to Abe. He began to talk to her….just a calm, tall stranger who, connecting her appearance with her statements, began to talk with her about the interesting artists he'd seen at the tattoo convention taking place at Renaissance Center. As several stops passed, he chatted with her about his favorite night spots in the city. By the time the People Mover arrived at her stop, she was calm and making polite conversation. This was witnessed by Abe's parents who were visiting Detroit. When asked where he'd learned this de-escalation skill, he told us that it is an essential tool for a bar owner.

———•———

There is a maple tree in front of the family home ("322") where Abe and Josh grew up. Every autumn, the leaves on that tree would turn vibrant yellow and fall to the ground, covering the front yard. The boys would gather the leaves into a large pile near the porch and jump off the porch into the leaf pile. Neighborhood friends would join in with many kids jumping off the porch into the leaves. Abe's cousin Carrie was there, but she was afraid to make the leap. She tenderly recalls Abe holding her hand and jumping with her.

In the years between the James-Michael Simmons Band and Josh's relocation to Lo Angeles, Josh and Abe Sulfaro performed as Brother, Inc. at Detroit casinos, Motor City and MGM Grand. Abe said he saw surprise of the faces of the panel when two white guys showed up to audition. Apparently the name Brother, Inc. had misled the judges who were expecting to hear some Motown from Black musicians. Reading the situation, the Sulfaro brothers broke into a Marvin Gaye tune. They were hired.

BROTHER INC.

Professional Musicians

ROCK • BLUES • DANCE

MODERN • CLASSIC

Josh Sulfaro • (734) 241-4389

tch5@provide.net

Abe's Aunt Bev still laughs when she tells of this encounter with her very young nephew who was attempting to make his Christmas wishes clear. He told her, "Please don't get me a shirt with a little 'arimal' on it." He was referring to the polo shirts being sold at that time with the retail store's emblem on the left front such as an alligator or a horse.

As described in the Epilogue of The Antiheroes, there was a gathering of Abe's friends at Reflections Bar & Grille in southwest Detroit a few months after his death. A large, bearded man shared this memory. He and Abe were at Reflections, and Abe had showed up wearing a dew rag on his head. The big guy said to Abe, "Man, you look like Aunt Jemima with that rag on your head." Abe replied, "I can take this rag off my head and I'm still Abe, but no matter what you take off, you're still fat." With that, the big guy stood up and lunged at Abe who ran out the back door. The big guy chased him down and tackled him in the parking lot, looking down at Abe from the top and saying, "Oh yeah? I might be fat, but I can still do this." Thinking of what he might do to get this hefty dude off the top of him, Abe raised his head and kissed the guy on the mouth, saying, "And I can still do this." That was all it took to free him from the clutches of a much larger adversary. The big man told this story with great affection and a smile on his face.

Artwork by Ryan Sulfaro

The house in northern Michigan where Abe's parents moved after his father's retirement from Ford Motor Company became a refuge for Abe whenever he could break away from the Nuclear Lounge. One Thanksgiving when he was with us, Aunt Bev and family friend Buffy Carr were invited to dinner. The table was set and dinner was served. Abe sat very briefly at the corner of the table, said hello to everyone and immediately excused himself to go for a walk in the woods with the dogs, leaving the gathering for Thanksgiving dinner without him. When he returned, we were all still at the table. He and the dogs walked past us without a word and went downstairs to the bedroom where he stayed, reading, until everyone was gone except Mom and Dad. When asked why he had been so antisocial, he replied, "I'd rather eat leftovers later. It tastes better and I'm a night guy."

Five phone calls from Abe when he was in college:

1. He needed something and didn't want to ask for it, so he pretended to be his brother Josh who was attending the same college. It worked.

2. As a freshman, he had taken a walk in Boston Commons in the winter and saw homeless people warming their hands over a burn barrel. Abe was distraught.

3. Called to say he was hungry and had been eating plain boiled macaroni. He was reminded that his meals had been paid for in the college cafeteria. The kid just didn't make time in his day for meals.

4. Called to ask us to send him some quarters because he needed to wash clothes in the college laundromat. Again, just not in touch with the mundane and had to be reminded that he could get change for dollars and that it would take several days in the mail and would be expensive to mail quarters to him.

5. Distraught again. Abe and his brother worked at the liquor store across the street from the college and knew the street folks by name, most of them begging for change to buy their next bottle and sleeping in the "T" (subway) tunnels. A homeless guy who had purchased a bottle of booze from Abe was found face-down, frozen to the street in front of the dormitory. From the window above, Abe watched the police pry him off the pavement.

As young men, Abe and Josh accompanied their dad on a couple of deer hunting trips to northern Michigan. When they arrived back at the cabin one evening, it was discovered that there were only two rifles rather than three. Truth is the gun was not important to Abe. He had no interest in killing a deer and was probably daydreaming or reading, his back against a tree all by himself...his preferred state. They returned to the woods in the dark with flashlights to retrieve Abe's gun.

As the golden years of the Goth life and the excitement at Detroit's City Club waned, Greg McFarland (Spam in The Antiheroes) became involved with a young woman who would later become the mother of three of his children. Being pulled toward a more domestic existence and at the same time preferring, like Abe, the lifestyle of an unentangled male, Greg was conflicted. Recognizing Greg's bidirectional pull between two incompatible lifestyles, Abe counseled him: "If you do this (settle down and have children), you've gotta do it balls in." Greg still cites this advice from a friend and brother who knew he stood to lose his sidekick during the greatest times of their lives. Abe's untitled poem in at the front of MEMOIRS de NOCTURNE echoes his deep sadness at the loss of their shared adventures, now with the dreaded premonition of his early demise.

Left, Abe   Right, Greg

Abe and Josh were always very close with mutual love and acceptance of each other's gifts as well as their differences. This anecdote is hilarious yet made us wonder if Abe had low self-esteem. Or, more likely, was it pride in his dark side? We were at the Detroit Jazz Festival, having a few drinks and feeling fine. At the time, Josh was living in Los Angeles. With a big smile, laughing, Abe said, "My brother is getting a little crunchy for me. You know...LA granola bar crunchy. He's Raisin Bran, two scoops of sunshine in every box. I'm Count Chocula with two black fangs."

An evening in Detroit with Abe during a visit by Josh from LA.
Left, Greg McFarland; Right, Josh Sulfaro

Detroit percussionist Dan Lewis remembers an abduction attempt that was thwarted by Abe, Josh, and Dan Oestrike of the James-Michael Simmons Band. Dan has cerebral palsy and was in a wheelchair in the audience at Armadillo's, a country bar and live music venue in Toledo, Ohio where JMS was performing. Dan noticed a man staring at him in a weird way, moving closer and closer until he was near enough to make physical contact, placing his hands on the wheelchair and saying, "You're coming with me." Dan began to try to fight this attempt, at the same time thinking he would be found dead in a ditch or an alley because the place was very loud and the dance floor packed between him and his friends in

JMS. From center stage, Abe saw Dan struggling and jumped off the stage in the middle of a song, yelling, "Someone's trying to take Dan!" Abe was followed by his brother Josh and Dan Oestrike. They charged the would-be abductor who ran. Dan Lewis credits Abe with saving his life that night during an action-packed interruption in the live music and line dancing.

Caption: Backstage at the Diamondback
Left to right-Dan Oestrike, Josh, Abe

In third grade, the students were assigned desk partners with two desks placed together face-to-face. Abe's desk partner was an overweight Black girl in a school where Blacks were not common in the 70s. At this young age, Abe was already a social justice warrior. He made it his responsibility to see that his desk partner, whose name remains etched into our memories, was included in all activities and treated equally among classmates.

Written into a memory book by Abe's Aunt Royetta at his wake at the Diamondback Saloon: "With our very limited knowledge of wine, Sally and I were standing in the kitchen discussing the merits of chianti. I said, 'I like that one with a knight on the label...maybe from Spain?' Then Abe's voice from the living room-- 'Gabbiano.' " This happened just a couple of weeks before he died. Royetta added to her note in the memory book, "Yes, Abe."

Another story from Dayve Disintegration: Abe and his friends were meeting their dates at a bar for drinks before to going to City Club. The guys arrived first in Goth attire and makeup. A man in a business suit began to challenge the Goth guys, aggressively questioning them about why they would dress this way. As Abe was calmly giving him the reasons for Goth subculture dress, explaining the differences between Goth and mainstream culture, the girls entered dressed to the Goth 9s in short skirts, fishnet stockings and corsets. Nodding toward the ladies coming through the door, Abe added, "And there are the main reasons." The confronter dropped his in-your-face challenges and ordered a round of drinks.

Left to right: Greg (Spam) McFarland, Abe, Dayve (Disintegration) Watson

---

Written by Abe's cousin Libby: "One of my favorite memories of Abe is from Hilary's (her sister's) wedding. I vividly remember standing on the deck outside while the reception was going on, listening for sounds of my twin boys who were outside with a sitter. Instead I heard laughter coming from a wooded area behind the parking lot. It got louder, and I watched Abe and Josh emerge from the yard, laughing together, sharing a story and a drink. I remember watching them and hoping my boys have a close relationships when they become adults, too. I also remember very fondly Abe's genuine interest in every new person I ever introduced to him—whether a friend, boyfriend or spouse. He was always attentive and thoughtfully inquisitive about their lives, making my loved ones feel welcome no matter how long between our visits. His genuine kindness showed me that he cared for me and I hope he could feel the love that I have for him as well."

Written at the wake by a neighborhood friend from the teenage years: "Abe, my brother. You remind me of laughter—you and me, bud. You used to take shit and turn it funny to the point of tears and my belly hurt from laughing so hard and for so long that we didn't even remember the shit that made us laugh to begin with. Excuse the sloppy writing. Me and Josh did a couple of shots of tequila and whiskey in your name. Love ya, Bro. Rest in peace. Tommy Notario"

Artist Quotes

...most artists create out of despair.
The very nature of creation is not a performing glory.
It's a painful, difficult search within.

Louise Berliawsky Nevelson

A cat's rage is beautiful, burning with pure cat flame,
all its hair standing up and crackling blue sparks, eyes blazing and sputtering.

William S. Burroughs

Artists live in unknown spaces
and give themselves over to following something unknown.

Kiki Smith

www.ingramcontent.com/pod-product-compliance
Lightning Source LLC
Chambersburg PA
CBHW020050170426
43199CB00009B/231